n Words

haw

Ozzy "*Talking*"

OMNIBUS PRESS

OZZY *Talking*

Cover & Book designed by Phil Gambrill @ Fresh Lemon.
Picture research by Nikki Lloyd & Steve Behan.

ISBN: 0.7119.9290.1
Order No: OP 48895

Exclusive Distributors:
Music Sales Limited,
8/9 Frith Street, London W1D 3JB, UK.

Music Sales Corporation,
257 Park Avenue South, New York, NY 10010, USA.

Macmillan Distribution Services,
53 Park West Drive, Derrimut, Vic 3030, Australia.

To the Music Trade only:
Music Sales Limited,
8/9 Frith Street, London W1D 3JB, UK.

Photo credits:
Front cover: Mick Hutson/Redferns. Back cover: London Features International.
All other pictures supplied by London Features International, Redferns, Big Pictures & Rex.

Every effort has been made to trace the copyright holders of the
photographs in this book but one or two were unreachable.
We would be grateful if the photographers concerned would contact us.

Printed by: Caligraving Limited, Thetford, Norfolk.

A catalogue record for this book is available from the British Library.

Visit Omnibus Press on the web at www.omnibuspress.com

The author would like to thank Nigel 'Nightingale' Cross,
Dave Ling and Nephele Headleand for their kind assistance

OZZY *Talking*

He's been described as a cross between Charlie Cairoli the circus clown and devil-worshipper Aleister Crowley, while he's had more women, done more dope'n'booze and lived life harder than just about any rock'n'roller still alive. Yet as he sails on into his sixth decade on earth, John Michael 'Ozzy' Osbourne, master showman and self-styled clown prince of darkness, is more alive and kickin' than some of the kids who worship him... and are less than half his age!

Introduction

The youngest member of a large blue-collar family in Aston, Birmingham, Ozzy was born on 3 December 1948 and, barely out of his teens, made his mark as the front man of hard-rock quartet Black Sabbath alongside guitarist Tony Iommi, bass player Terry 'Geezer' Butler and drummer Bill Ward. Over ten years and half a dozen or so albums, Sabbath almost single-handedly invented the term 'heavy metal'. Their self-styled Satanic image was always tongue-in-cheek, but their brain-crunching 1970 anthem 'Paranoid' has gone down as one of the greatest rock songs ever recorded.

Never taken seriously at the time by either their record labels or the critics, Sabbath's riff-dominated, black-hearted rock found immediate favour with the kids who bought their records by the million. However, by the end of the Seventies as Sabbath fell into a mire of drug addiction and management problems, Ozzy was ousted from the band he helped start.

Down but not out, Ozzy's flagging career was swiftly turned around by Sharon Arden, who became his manager and then his wife. Hooking up with American guitar-wizard Randy Rhoads, Ozzy was soon back on top with a clutch of well-received solo albums, most notably *Blizzard Of Ozz* and *Diary Of A Madman*. Rhoads tragically died in a plane accident in 1982 and, in the aftermath, Ozzy's life once again began to spiral out of control.

While the new breed of Eighties bands like Metallica paid lip service to the influence of Sabbath, Ozzy's fortunes were as mixed as those of his former mates who'd kept the Sabbath name going through thick and thin. More Ozzy bands and solo albums came and went. The American moral majority railed at his ever-increasing outrageous stage antics and proclamations, and he was subpoenaed when his lyrics were cited as having been directly to blame for the death of a young fan, though the case was eventually thrown out of court. Ozzy, meanwhile, scooped a Grammy for Best Vocal in a Metal Song for 'No More Tears'.

Going on the wagon for good in 1991, the man who once admitted he had actually enjoyed working in an abattoir even turned over a new leaf as a vegetarian! And this monster of rock, whose legendary feats include allegedly biting the head off a live bat and urinating on Texas's greatest monument, the Alamo, is still centre stage. With grunge bands like Nirvana singing his praises, Ozzy founded the OzzFest, a Lollapalooza-style touring operation showcasing the best new hard-rock bands across America. It is now regarded as having put the life back into heavy metal!

Never one to sit on his backside, the Double O ended the millennium in harness with original Black Sabbath bandmates Tony, Geezer and Bill for another crack at the big time, their first reunion (Live Aid aside) since 1979. A string of sell-out performances and a 1998 live album, *Reunion*, preceded a spell of studio activity, but the demands of a solo career saw Ozzy back on the road in his own right in late 2001 alongside Rob Zombie in the Merry Mayhem Tour, promoting his 24th consecutive US gold album *Down To Earth*. The fact that Osbourne played on through the pain barrier for days after sustaining a stress fracture of the leg – in the shower, of all places – confirmed that there were plenty of pages left to be added to the Diary of a Madman. And there was surely no better person to write 'em...

INTRODUCTION ,,

 **OZZY** *Talking*

Midland Maniac

JOHN OSBOURNE'S FORMATIVE YEARS IN BIRMINGHAM

"My earliest memory is of the Queen's Coronation Day, when my father dressed me up as a minstrel and I wouldn't have the black paint on my face. It was for a street party. And going to school for the first time. I fucking hated it and I didn't learn a damned thing. I just used to make everyone laugh." **1997**

"I had one pair of socks, never wore underwear, one pair of pants and one jacket – and that was it." 1998

"We used to have sing-songs in the house. That's probably why I sing like I do, I picked it up from my father and he'd only sing when he was pissed." **2001**

"I wasn't a particularly hard kid but I was the friend of the school bully. I always said that if you couldn't beat 'em, entertain them and do anything to get 'em on your side. That's where I started to show off." 1986

"I came from a very working-class family. Education was minimal. I later found out that I suffered from ADD and that I'm extremely dyslexic, but back in those days you were just called 'thick'. I left school less educated than when I started." **2001**

"I always felt inferior to everybody else. I was always just 'less'. Kids are cruel so they would taunt me about not being able to read. And the teachers were bastards – they knew something was up but couldn't be arsed to help me 'cos there were 40 other kids who, like me, probably didn't give a shit about being there anyway. We were all just doing time waiting to get out to the big world and earn some money." 2001

"When I was a kid, I always seemed to be obsessed with the war and used to think Germany was miles and miles away. I thought about those planes comin' all that way to bomb Britain when it was only an hour-and-a-bit by air!" 1989

"I don't know why I'm into Germany so much. I think it must be that whole 1930s/1940s war period. I'm just drawn to it. Not because of the Nazis or anything. I went to see that film, *Hope And Glory*, and it brought me back to my childhood. I could really relate to the whole era." 1989

"My dad worked at the GEC plant in Witton and my mum was working at the Lucas assembly shop. God only knows how they managed to bring us all up. There was never much money about, but they never let me or my brothers and sisters go without essentials. It used to tear me apart seeing my mother crying because she hadn't got enough money to spend on bills and things." 1986

MIDLAND MANIC

"My father always used to say to me, 'You've got to learn a trade.' And my mother would say for years, 'When are you going to pack up this rock'n'roll nonsense and get a proper job?' Still does. When I was 17 I thought, 'I know what'll please my Dad.' I tried to join the Army. I had a tap around my neck on a string for jewellery, I was wearing a pyjama top and my backside was hanging out. The guy said, 'No thank you. We want subjects, not objects.' I said, 'I'll be the target. Just give me the job.' But he wouldn't." 1994

"I never really left Birmingham before Sabbath. The first time I actually did was on holiday to my aunt's house in Sunderland. That was the very first time I saw the ocean, when I was 14... what a shithole that was! Abysmal, cold, this fishy smell everywhere." 1989

"My first tattoo is on my arm and it says 'OZZY'. I had it done when I was 14. I went home and showed it to my father... he kicked the shit out of me!" 1997

"I had numerous (jobs)... builders, plumbers, slaughtering, butchering. I worked in a mortuary for about a week. I was fucking mad. I'd do anything, and nothing would phase me. When I worked at the abattoir, all I did for the first two weeks was throw up, but I soon got over that little problem." 1990

"One of the worst jobs was tuning car horns in a soundproof room. There were ten of us tuning something like 1,500 horns each a day, and the noise was fucking unbelievable. Working in an abattoir killing sheep and cows was much better." 1997

"There was a giant mountain of sheep's stomachs, and my job was to get this knife and cut them up and empty the puke out of the stomachs. I was so tired of throwing up, my eyes were bulging out of head from straining. Everyone who eats meat should walk through an abattoir. You will not make four steps without puking your guts out. I guarantee." 2001

"I never could conform to a system. When I worked at Lucas tuning car horns I remember saying to this guy Harry, how long have you been working here? And he got all proud of himself, '35 years come this summer, and I get this gold watch when I retire'. I thought if I want a fucking gold watch that bad, I'll go and break a jeweller's window and run off with one. I watched the system kill my father – he worked in a factory all his life, retired and died within a year." 1989

"I was heartbroken when my father died, but at least he saw that I had made something of a success of my life. That meant a lot to me." 1982

"I fell into a life of crime. I started by robbing a clothes shop at the back of our house. When I broke in a second time I was caught." 1986

"I was the Norman Wisdom of burgling. I did everything wrong, like wearing gloves with the fingers out." 1989

MIDLAND MANIC

OZZY *Talking*

"As a kid I was a ruffian – a real tearaway. I tried all kinds of jobs but ended up as a professional burglar. One day I got caught breaking into a house and was sent to prison. It was a real lesson to me. After that I got together with the other lads to form a band. Music saved me from becoming a hardened criminal." 1982

"I used to work with this Irish guy... he used to go and clock houses, find out when people went to work, then we'd burgle them. This time the idiot didn't realise the house he was watching was a boarding house. People had gone to work but the owner was on night shift and was still in bed. When we broke in he beat seven shades of shit out of us. I got three months – it was burglary, larceny, assault and possessing dope all in one thing. Mind you, I was on the run at the time so I quite liked the nick – free food, free tobacco. It was heaven to me 'cos I'd had no dough. I shared a cell with a murderer. He used to tell me the ways he'd killed people. I quite got into it at the time." 1981

"When I was in nick, I never remembered the downers – only the good laughs we had sometimes, but I wouldn't like to go back there again. I like my freedom... I had nothing to do inside. You did about two hours' work a day and the rest of the time you were locked in your cell. That's when I did my tattoos – with a sewing needle and tins of grate polish." 1982

"Did I learn anything in prison? Yeah, not to go back. I was a kid at the time (1965) and I was only away for seven weeks. It was for something as pathetic as non-payment of fines after this burglary I'd been charged with. I only broke into the house to be one of the boys. Jail scared the life out of me." 1998

"I was 17 and pissed off when I tried to join the Army. I wanted to see the world and shoot as many people as possible – which is not much different from being in a rap band these days! They just told me to fuck off." 2000

"My father gave me an aluminium crucifix – we couldn't afford gold then – and later I got it copied in gold. I don't wear it all the time though – it's that big you could crucify yourself on it, and I look like a tinker when I'm laden down with diamonds and gold." **2001**.

"'My mother and sisters still call me John, but my wife and kids call me Ozzy. If I'm walking down the street and someone shouts John, I don't turn around. I was thinking of changing my name but I never got round to it." 1998

"One day I got asked to step in for rehearsals for a mate's band, I daren't do the gig itself but I realised then that I could sing of sorts. My first gig was at Birmingham fire station, to an audience of four fire buckets and a drunken fireman. I came in and almost passed out with fear. My father loaned me the money to get a PA and a microphone." **2001**

"The first gig I ever went to was about '67, I saw Carl Wayne & The Vikings – who later became The Move – at a polytechnic in Birmingham." 2001

OZZY STRANGLING ZAKK WYLDE! **MIDLAND MANIC**

Musical Influences

HOW ROCK'N'ROLL SOOTHED THE SAVAGE BEAST

"I loved music as a child – the magic behind rock'n'roll. My sisters would bring home Chuck Berry records, and I would sing and dance around the house. At night I would lie awake and fantasise about doing something great." 1998

"My first rock festival was the Woburn Abbey Music Festival in 1966. Jimi Hendrix was on the bill. My mates and I ended up burning a fucking shed down 'cos we were so cold." 1998

JIMI HENDRIX

"I never ever thought I would become anything or do much at all. The Beatles gave me a seed of fantasy. That was my ticket out of there. To want to do something. The weirdest thing of it all was that it happened." 2001

"It was hearing 'She Loves You' that did it for me. For people my age, where I'm from, it wasn't albums that changed your life – it was singles, because that's

what you could buy. 'She Loves You' was the first record I ever bought. I was 13 went down Witton Road in Aston. It changed everything. 2001

"I really, really wanted to become a Beatle. When they played the *Thank Your Lucky Stars* TV show at Alpha TV studios in Birmingham I went down to see them and you couldn't get near the place from half a mile out. It wasn't just about the sheer number of people it was the atmosphere – Beatlemania. With the emphasis on the mania. It was special and it changed my life. There will never be another Elvis, Roy Orbison or Beatles. Ever."
2001

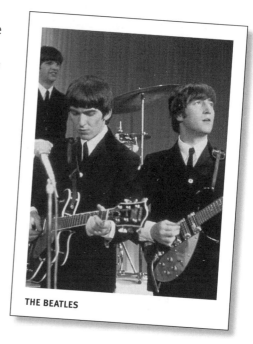

THE BEATLES

" My all-time favourite albums are *Revolver* and *Sgt Pepper* by The Beatles, Wings' *Band On The Run* and *Imagine* by John Lennon. You couldn't release an album called *Revolver* these days – you'd be run out of town." 2001

PAUL McCARTNEY

"I've never met a Beatle. I've flown with Paul McCartney but I didn't want to impose because I would have felt like a dickhead. He was with Linda and they didn't come near me because of, you know, the bat thing." **2001**

MUSICAL INFLUENCES "

Sabbath Lives!

SEEDS OF A SUPERGROUP

"The whole hippy thing was still happening around that time, and for us that was bullshit. We lived in a dreary, polluted, dismal town in Birmingham, and were angry about it – and that was reflected in our music." **1998**

"You gotta think of the time! It was all this fucking bells and hippies and smoking dope and free love shit and we just thought, 'It ain't like that, really.' When you're living in Birmingham and it's fucking raining every day and you've got no money in your pocket and you get this bullshit – that just wasn't right to us."

1997

"I lived in Aston and my Dad was fucking dying of industrial pollution. What the fuck did I care about fucking flowers and that hippy shit? All that pretty pretty stuff. People were going round singing shit like, 'If you're going to fucking San Francisco, make sure you're wearing a flower in your hair.' Well the only flower you saw in Aston was on a fucking gravestone." **1997**

"In those days if you had a PA system, you were accepted as a singer whether you could sing or not, because nobody could afford the equipment." 1998

❝I was in a band called Rare Breed with Geezer Butler, and Tony and Bill were in a band in Cumbria called Mythology. When they broke up, Tony came back to Birmingham looking for a singer and a bass player, and I'd put an advert in a music shop. Geezer was playing rhythm with Rare Breed, but switched to bass and we formed a band called Earth, playing jazz/blues...Ten Years After kind of stuff.❞

1990

❝When we started the record companies didn't want to know. They wouldn't even take the trouble to listen to our tapes to see if we were any good. We were dismissed point blank. And we went through some really bad times.❞ 1970

❝We were called Earth at the time; we used to rehearse across the road from a movie theatre, and there was a horror film on. And Tony says, 'Isn't it weird that people pay money to see a horror film? Why don't we make scary music?' It came just like that! We never thought it was for real. I remember when we started getting invites to black masses, we all looked at each other and said, 'Is this for real or what?'❞ 1997

❝There was one time when Bill and me couldn't go out at the same time. Somehow we'd ended up only having one pair of shoes between us and we had to take it in turns to go out.❞

❝It scared us. When we first played the Marquee we were all nervous. We thought London was so big we could die and nobody would notice.❞ 1970

SABBATH LIVES!

"The Star Club (in Hamburg) was hard work, all right. It wasn't only the amount of work you had to get through. When The Beatles were talking about five sets a night, they weren't joking. We used to go on and off that stage like jacks in a box. It just seemed to go on forever. I had the feeling they didn't care what we were doing on stage as long as *something* was going on. If we stopped or anything they used to go mad."

"I asked myself, 'Why is there a line of people with money in their hands, paying to get the shit scared out of them?' It's because people like to get a thrill out of being around evil." 1998

"No matter how much you'd tell these people it's not for real, they'd go 'Oh yeah, but we know' and wink. Even 'NIB' on the first album was a humorous song about the Devil falling in love, and I thought it was *hysterical*! But nobody got the point!" 1997

"I remember doing a gig years ago in Memphis. Every time we played there, all the equipment would blow up for some reason. On this occasion we pulled out of the gig and I went to my hotel room. There were about 15 freaks outside my door with black-painted faces and robes and daggers and candles. I slammed the door and phoned the roadie. I said: 'There are a load of cuckoo brains out there.'
"The roadie got them all round with their candles, said 'Happy Birthday', blew the candles out and told them to clear off. I used to get people like that sleeping in corridors outside my room wherever we went. They got into the literal side of Black Sabbath, searching out meanings." 1980

"When we got to America the manager said to us, 'They've had a procession for you in San Francisco.' We just thought, 'What the fuck?' It was that Anton LaVey guy who had this fucking carnival with this white Rolls-Royce and people dancing in the streets. We didn't realise who Anton LaVey was. We didn't know he was a fucking high priest of black magic or whatever." 1997

❝When we came out of *The Exorcist* we had to stay in one room together – that's how black magic we were.❞

❝We've never got into an ego thing. Why should we? People inflict ego trips on a band. We're just ordinary people. Black Sabbath is the tightest friendship thing I've ever encountered. And we're just beginning to get into a richer musical thing.❞ 1972

❝I go out on stage and I think, 'Fuck it man, all we are anyway is a rock'n'roll band.' I just can't stand to see a band on stage trying to baffle the audience. I've been to the Marquee and seen groups and they're just playing bollocks, man, complete and utter rubbish. And the kids... you can see them looking and thinking, 'Wow, man, I don't dig this but it must be good.' They go, 'Hip hip hooray, Peace...' And all that shit. When I go on stage I want to get people to dance. I don't want people to think this is an A minor or a D, F sharp...❞ **1972**

❝I just did it to them one day and they all did it back!❞
1975, ON THE INFAMOUS FOREFINGER-LITTLE FINGER PEACE SIGNS AT GIGS

THE CLASSIC BLACK SABBATH LINE UP...
(L-R) OZZY, BILL WARD, GEEZER BUTLER, TONY IOMMI

SABBATH LIVES!

OZZY *Talking*

❝What's this sudden cult-fucking-god vibe? We were just four guys from Birmingham that couldn't even write our own names playing raw fucking music.❞ **1992**

❝**We were dimbos from Birmingham, we didn't fucking know. From having two bob in your pocket to a hundred quid was a big jump for us – we didn't know it should've been a fucking thousand quid.❞** 1990

❝We had money to burn and booze coming out of our ears.❞ **1998**

❝**If people can come to a Sabbath gig or listen to a Sabbath record and get rid of their aggressions, that's great. If they're miserable they can put on a Black Sabbath record and think that the band knows how they feel. They've got something they can relate to. It's great to see kids at our gigs enjoying themselves and not kicking shit out of each other.❞** 1975

❝What a fucking drag that is. We opened (in Portsmouth) with 'Paranoid' as usual and suddenly the place went potty. There were

kids rushing down the front and girls screaming and grabbing us. We couldn't believe it – it was just like the teenybopper era all over again. We don't need fans like those. But we'll just have to grin and bear them and they'll go away. We're not changing our stage act to please the kids who just bought the single.❞
1970, IN THE WAKE OF 'PARANOID' GOING TOP 10

❝**The reason we appeal to so many people so instantly is because our sound is good and basic. It doesn't take a lot of understanding.**

The impact is right there. Of course we were choked off with the reviews and we began to wonder if we had done the right thing. But we had a tremendous hardcore following in places like Carlisle and Workington in the early days and they were the ones who bought our album when it came out. I guess the others followed out of curiosity when they saw it in the charts." 1970

❝It's just the excitement, it's just the feeling you can't beat it. It's like a drug –you wanna get back up as soon as you can.❞ **1975**

❝**I tried working with other guys, but these days bands haven't got it together as much as they used to have. The first thing they want to talk about is money which is really the last thing that concerns me. My view is that if you've got enough bread to scrape by on, then you're alright. I missed the family atmosphere of Black Sabbath. I had a rest, but knew in my heart that I was making a mistake and I just had to get back in there.❞**

1978, ON HIS FIRST – ALBEIT TEMPORARY – SPLIT FROM SABBATH IN 1977

❝I always got off on the people that came to see Sabbath, but the whole thing turned into a monstrosity at the end of it. The reason I left wasn't because I fell out with any of the guys. I think the world of those guys, I really do. I just could never stay with a job if something was bugging me. It affects me in all ways. I got out before I started hating anybody. There's a couple of guys on the Sabbath road crew that I can't stand and I should never have allowed that to bother me, but it did.

❝It's all supposed to be about family, so it's affected me. I hate fat serfs that just gloat at your success and then try to be part of you.

SABBATH LIVES!

The beginning of the end for me came after *Sabbath Bloody Sabbath*. I just didn't get off on the last few albums. We couldn't reproduce what we were doing in the studio 'cos it was so overdubbed with 300 voices and all that. Tony would do seven guitar overdubs and I felt like I had to compete in a way to stay part of it... it was so bizarre... multi-tracking voices and backward harmonies... drowning people's brains with all this scientific bullshit I don't understand." 1978

Deep down inside I wanted to leave Sabbath three years ago, but I didn't 'cos of the loyalty thing. I used to feel inadequate because I didn't play an instrument and couldn't contribute on a musical level. But what I *could* do was make it with the audience..." 1978

It's been like a holiday. It's given me a lot of time to think and although I'd been trying to work with other musicians, it was very difficult. After nine years with the same people you get used to things. When they rang up to ask me if I'd come back, I knew there was only one answer." 1978

We had some good laughs, sure – especially with Bill. He was always good for a crack, but Geezer was forever moaning about how he wanted to take a year's holiday as soon as possible. And Tony was kind of difficult to get on with. He used to be quiet for hours and then he'd suddenly do something mad which he thought was funny. I mean once he set fire to Bill's beard which was really dangerous. But Bill was great... he just breathed in this big cloud of fumes and said 'Hmmmmm – a good smoke, that.'" 1980, ON HIS FIRST SPELL WITH SABBATH

Sabbath: The Music

OZZY'S THOUGHTS ON CLASSIC BLACK SABBATH

"We didn't slaughter a first-born son on the tape machine. We just got as pissed as farts." **1997**

"Sabbath is aggressive music for angry people." 1997

"I don't dig progressive rock at all. It just never turned me on. I must be a nutcase but I just get pissed off and bored with it all. I dig Humble Pie. If you can stamp your feet to it and nod your head, it's good as far as I'm concerned. It's good old rock'n'roll and God bless it man, because that's what it's all about for me." **1972**

"I can honestly tell you, there was no inner secret, no fuckin' black magic. It was just four guys doing whatever they could."

"Sabbath was a reaction against all these stupid bands around at the time going on about young love and boy-meets-girl. It seemed to us this was more like real life." **1976**

"I liked the name Black Sabbath because of the succession of vowel sounds." 1970

OZZY *Talking*

"We started writing heavy riffs, wrote the song 'Black Sabbath' and then we changed our name. I would come up with the vocal line, Geezer would come up with the lyrics, and Tony was mainly the man who came up with the riffs. Whatever anybody says about Tony Iommi, he is the master of fucking riffs. We never realised at the time how fucking clever he was." 1990

"A few weeks ago I was in my studio playing some of the Sabbath CDs, thinking, I wonder what these'll sound like? The fuckin' timings that we used to do were fuckin' weird. Weird fuckin' drum patterns, weird vocals – how the fuck we came up with it I'll never know."

"One thing everyone has to understand about Black Sabbath's lyrics. They're not downer lyrics, they're just telling everybody where it's at. That's all it is. People must think we sleep off rafters with wings on our backs, every night, taking reds and drinking wine. We see a lot and we write about what we see. We have a couple of songs about people getting stoned, but so have a lot of people. It's a heavy, doomy thing but it's what we see.

"Love wouldn't go with the style of music we play. It would be like going to see *Frankenstein* with the *Sound Of Music* soundtrack behind it." 1975

"My old man used to say, 'You've got to give people a tune so they've got something to sing after they've had a few pints of Newcastle Brown and it's cold by the bus stop.' Sabbath might be heavy, but there's always the melody in there that makes us what we are." 2001

The First LP (Black Sabbath)

"We were on our way to do a residency in the Hershey Club in Zurich, and on our way down to the ferry (we were a day early), we recorded the first album in 12 hours, then got back in the van and went to

Switzerland. We played it virtually live, with a couple of overdubs here and there, on two four-track machines. It cost about two grand, and it still sells to this day. **"** **1990**

"When we did the first album, it wasn't like we sat around a fucking campfire fucking burning virgins at the stake or anything. " 1997

"We recorded our first album in 12 hours or so on two four-track machines and straight after fucked off to a six-week residency in a fuckin' Swiss cafe. Then all of a sudden we were megastars. What? It was like somebody had flipped a coin.**"**

"I remember when the first album came out I thought, 'Great, I can show my dad.' We put it on the old radiogram and I remember him looking at mum with this really confused look on his face and turning to me and saying, 'Son, are you sure you're just drinking the occasional beer?'" 2000

"If a wizard walked up to you, you'd definitely go 'Fuck me, there's a wizard!'**"**

1997, ON 'THE WIZARD'

Paranoid

"A lot of *Paranoid* was left over from *Black Sabbath*, though the actual song 'Paranoid' was written in the studio because we needed three and a half minutes to fill the album – we just went in and jammed that one out. The best songs always happen that way –

you can sit down and plan and fucking work it out, but it's those quickies that turn out the best.

❝The original title of the album was *War Pigs*, as you can see from the guy with the crash helmet and shield on the cover. I dunno who that was, I'd love to meet the guy, I bet he's a great big, fat, middle-aged fucking rent collector now.❞ 1990

❝... I can't believe it. I just don't understand its success. But I suppose it's a 'standard' – like Free's 'All Right Now' – every time there's a record slump it's pushed out again and it seems to sell. Considering we recorded it in three-and-a-half minutes, it's not bad!❞ 1980, ON THE 'PARANOID' SINGLE REISSUE

❝'Iron Man' is about a guy who invents a time machine and finds the world is coming to an end. He comes back and turns to iron and people won't listen to him. They think he's not real. He goes a bit barmy and decides to get his revenge by killing people. He tries to do good, but in the end it turns into bad.❞ 1982

❝If you can frighten people with words, it's better than letting them find out by trying drugs.❞ 1982

Master Of Reality

❝We went into the recording studio and thought, 'You play into a microphone and someone tape-records it.' We never knew we could stick different effects on it and everything.❞ 1996

❝I think *Master Of Reality* was a great album. Nobody would dare to do what we were doing and get away with it. We defied all fuckin' realms of commerciality and got accepted. People sometimes overlook what the times were like when we did those first three records. It was all lovey-dovey bullshit, you know.❞

1998

Black Sabbath Volume 4

❝We wanted to call it *Snowblind* with all the obvious references, but the record company wouldn't let us. That's why it became *Volume 4* and they shoved a copy of my 'boat' on there. If you listen to that track ('Snowblind') you'll hear me whisper 'cocaine' after each verse. Originally, I said it out loud but the record company made us take it off. On the cover there's a special thanks to the great 'COKE-Cola' company, which was our way of getting that reference on there. We were doing tons of the fucking stuff.❞ 1997

❝**This album has lots of short tracks for variety. Long numbers get boring. If we want to retain our popularity we will have to make a change. We're getting some weird effects in the studio and doing insane things. For instance, we got everybody to march to the top of this big staircase the other day, singing like the Seven Dwarfs. It was amazing. Everyone letting themselves go, and we took it down on tape.❞** 1972

OZZY'S BAND FOR HIS 1980 *BLIZZARD OF OZZ* TOUR AND ALBUM...
(L-R) BOB DAISLEY, OZZY, LEE HERSLAKE, RANDY RHOADS

“When we did that album, it was like one big Roman orgy – we were in the jacuzzi all day doing coke, and every now and again, we'd get up to do a song.” **1998**

“We called the shots, and if producers didn't like it then we fucking beat the shit out of them.” 1997

“When I think about those records, I remember the time we had when we were making them. That's why I like *Volume 4* (1972). We'd got the rock-star fever by then – limousines everywhere, groupies sucking our dicks, dealers dropping by with bags of white powder.” **1998**

Sabbath Bloody Sabbath

“The title track was something about the word 'God' and changing it all around. Instead of 'God bless all of you', it was 'Bog blast all of you'. Geezer Butler wrote those words and he was very fucking stoned. He *must* have been.” **1997**

“Geezer's an incredible lyricist. Not many people know he wrote 90 per scent of the lyrics for Sabbath. I'll never forget when he wrote the lyrics to 'Spiral Architect'. I was on the phone and I asked him if he had the lyrics for me to sing yet. He says to me, 'Got a pen?' He started off, 'Sorcerers of madness, selling me the sun...' And I go, 'You're fucking reading this out of a book. You're joking!' My mouth dropped open.” 1995

“With Sabbath we used to get so fucked up and stoned and that and spend the whole day jamming. We had tapes running for days, then we'd pick pieces out and puzzle it all together.” **1990**

OZZY *Talking*

Sabotage

"By the time we did *Sabotage* (1975) we were all fucked up with drugs and we discovered we'd been viciously ripped off by our management. And that cover is *horrible*. Bill has got his wife's tights on with my checked underpants underneath and I'm dressed up like a homo in a kimono. But you've got to understand the times – it was the Seventies, there was no MTV, no one to guide us..." **1998**

"We used to record the earlier stuff and go. Then they used to mix it and they'd add ridiculous effects, which was stupid to us because we didn't want them in. It's like me recording somebody else, and I mix the record the way I want it to sound and it's not my music! *Sabbath Bloody Sabbath* was an experiment, it was the first time we'd ever actually produced a record and the first time we had anything to do with the technical side.

"We've tried to keep it as basic as possible so we can reproduce it on stage. There's an instrumental that Tony wrote where we used the London Chamber Choir. It sounds like one of those epic bloody *Ben Hur* themes." 1975

"We'd like to put out a single, but you've got to be out-and-out pop. It's very hard to put something into three and a half minutes without sounding ridiculous. 10CC are the only band that are capable of doing that. We're not given the chance. When we put a single out the BBC goes 'ooooh!' They don't like us. They keep banning our lyrics because they're either about drugs, politics, the BBC or the stars at night." **1975**

"I remember being stuck in Miami with no dough during this album. We called the label to get more money and they sent us a telegram saying, 'Don't worry – the hamburgers are on the way!' Sick fucking joke. It wasn't a happy time, although when Tony came up with the riff to 'Superstar', it fucking pinned my ears back. I was *gobsmacked*." 1997

"In the end I felt like calling it *Crossroads* (a popular TV soap opera from Birmingham) and having Meg Richardson star in it. Every time there was a session we used to call it Chapter 99 – 'Will Black Sabbath complete the album this time?' It was like a bizarre nightmare sometimes but other times it was fun, especially the times we started throwing custard pies at each other. At the end of it, I was very confused because I had heard so much of it so I had to leave it alone for some time.

"When I heard it again, at first hearing I *hated* it. I realised that because of the constant work on it I'd built this barrier in my head, but I'm really satisfied now." 1975

"To me, *Sabotage* beats the last album – but I still have a liking for the last one. The last album was our first album really because we had got into the studio production thing and it takes a couple of albums to get into that. You go through all the experiments of banging dustbin lids and running herds of cattle through the studio to find out what that sounds like." 1975

"Doing 'Am I Going Insane?' exorcised the feelings in me. I don't think I'm going mad any more but I'm still angry – I've *always* been angry." 1976

SABBATH: THE MUSIC

Technical Ecstasy

" It's a good album. It was enjoyable to make – well, Tony enjoyed it! He made it... we used to write songs about how lousy the world is and it was right for the time. But now we know that everyone knows the world is bad so we've changed our approach. We're telling people stories in our music these days, I only hope they enjoy them... we don't see each other as much as we did before. "

" We didn't go into the studios with the intention of definitely changing. We just added a keyboard player to all our tracks. As a four-piece we were very limited. It got to the point where onstage we couldn't really get away with what we were doing in the studio – because we were making variations on the album, we were doing a fair amount of overdubbing. Whereas now we can virtually play onstage what we do in the studio...

" This album is like when the laxative has worked and you've just got it all out and you're all right again... it's like being constipated for two years and you've got rid of it. You've just got it out of your system. It's taken two years to get it all out and the crap we were going through has gone now. " 1976

" *Technical Ecstasy* was compared to Queen's *Night At The Opera* 'cos it was such a big production number. I mean, Queen openly admitted they took a lot of their ambition from Black Sabbath and there we were trying to get off Queen what they were trying to get off us or something! Why couldn't we be leaders any more? I'll tell you why. 'Cos we all became so content with it, so bored that we just got lazy, that's why. It seems to me that the names Black Sabbath and *Technical Ecstasy* were diametrically opposed to each other... nobody thought about it. I just didn't give a shit! I would go in there loaded every day, and in the end I felt guilty 'cos I abused what we had... " 1978

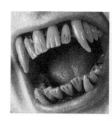

Never Say Die

❝We had a few internal
problems. My father was
dying, so that put us out
for over three months with
the funeral and everything.
I left the band for three
months before we got
back together to record it.
It's a combination of what
we've been through in
the last ten because
British blues – John
Mayall and Fleetwood
Mac – was the thing at the time.
We were into a 12-bar trip and early Ten Years After-style stuff.
So it's part of that trip. Then there's the heavy thing and the rock
thing. It's not just steamhammer head-banging stuff all the way
through… we got rid of our frustrations, what each of us
individually wanted to put down over the years but couldn't
because of the pressures of work.❞ 1978

Live At Last

❝… the live album is the biggest bunch of crap I've ever heard in my
life. I accept no responsibility for it, it's got nothing to do with me.
I feel like a dead prostitute – dig me up and fuck me one more
time. I feel so bad about it that I think if the deal was right I would
get back together with Sabbath and do one last show with them
so's we could make an official live album. We owe it to the kids.
This one needs melting down and making into Biro pens or
something.❞ 1980

Sabbath:
The Critical Legacy

"A group gets on and people help them, but when you reach a certain level they start to slam you. Before they were slamming us, they were slamming Led Zeppelin. Sometimes I get annoyed about it when criticism has no point, when it's not constructive. On the whole we grin and bear it, but I don't see why we should be knocked all the time... we strongly believe in our music. We don't do it because we like being pop stars." **1971**

"To be quite honest, I've lived with the press slagging us off for such a long time I'm quite used to it. Everyone's got their own opinion. It's them out there that matter to me. I'm not just doing it for the press. Nobody likes a bad slam. After you've been working all your merry hours in the studio, nobody likes a stab in the back from the press, but I suppose they're critics and if they weren't critics they wouldn't criticise. That's their job to knock a few holes into things." 1975

"It's because we're anti-hip and we don't want to know all that crap. For a time I did my damnedest to make these people happy, but they took the piss out of me for that. They must think we're dumb. But a lot of people who were writing these things about Sabbath aren't reporting ten years later. They're sweeping the streets or they're doormen at some poxy club somewhere.

"I would prefer 10,000 kids to get rid of their aggressions in one-and-a-half hours by watching me jumping up and down on a stage like a maniac than walk the streets and beat people over the head for their purse." **1978**

OZZY *Talking*

❝We didn't get time to think. We used to come off tour suffering from jet lag. We overdid the States, we OD'd on the States, like having a bad trip. It made us feel the recording side of the job was just another chore. The structure of the album is the backbone of the band. We got pretty sick and tired of being shoved around from one place to another like battery hens and going through the motions to an extent we got bored with each other.

❝We needed a break, we needed to think about music. We're led to believe that people want us to go back there. This is the biggest gamble of our lives. We've had quite a long time off and we haven't forgotten them... I hope they haven't forgotten us.❞ 1975

❝We were so out of it all the time, that we were incapable of making a solid decision between us. We were easy pickings for the vultures of rock'n'roll.❞ **1988**

❝It's only now I realise what an influence we were at the time. You look at all these punk things – we were, at the time of coming out, a new thing, I think. We said a lot in our music. We obviously must have affected a lot of people's minds or we wouldn't be doing it after ten years. There's a thousand monster acts that have come up in the last ten years like bats out of hell and disappeared into the history of rock never to be seen again. Died or fizzled out or OD'd or whatever. But we're still doing it. It makes me feel kind of proud.❞ 1978

❝We never knew what the fuck we were about. I never ever thought we were very good to be honest. 'Iron Man' and 'Paranoid' were good riffs but we weren't a great band. We were always fucked up on drugs and booze, every single day was fucked. The whole thing is actually a bit of a haze to me... anything bad that happened we never took seriously because we just went off down the pub and got pissed again. We missed out on a lot of reality.❞

❝When I listen to the records I made years ago with Black Sabbath they sound as if they're covered in mud from a Colombian volcano!❞ 1989

Out Of The Darkness

SINGER & SABS: THE PARTING OF THE WAYS

"There was nothing else I really wanted to do. I couldn't see myself getting a job behind a bar. I was a burglar before I joined Black Sabbath. I got caught seven times, and I had my taste of porridge. I thought well, if I'm not doing rock'n'roll, I'll be in prison. And I just didn't fancy going back for a striped sun-tan...

"In the early days it was all for one and one for all. In the end it was everybody for themselves. It got bitchy and catty. They were probably glad when I left because I was just a lunatic. I wasn't into it. I've no hard feelings now, although I was bitter at first. I wanted to leave for years before I did, but I wasn't prepared to own up to the rest of the band. I didn't want to give up the success and recognition." **1980**

"It's like a fucking divorce, that's what it is." 1979

"I heard from a good source yesterday that they've already started booking a tour out as Black Sabbath. That really got right up my fucking nose, that did. I own a quarter of the name and I wasn't notified or anything And I think they're really robbing the kids – conning them. If you bought a ticket to go and see The Rolling Stones and you get there and it's just Bill Wyman and a bunch of strangers, how would you feel? Let's face it, it's a totally different band.

"I think it's cheap what they're doing – the kids have always been loyal to us. When I found out last night I went nuts – hence one wrecked hotel room. It's over now – finished. It's a funny thing, but to me Sabbath is dead and I don't want no part of it."

❝I started to get the doubts in the pit of my stomach two years ago – it really ended for me then.❞ 1979

❝The last couple of albums were very trying for me. This time it is permanent. It's not like I'm going back at the last minute. I definitely don't want to work with them again. After 11 years I think I deserve a better crack of the whip than I did get. When I came off the tour I had a phone call from somebody saying that Tony was going to leave the band, that we'd had an argument or something. So I phoned Tony up and said, 'Have I upset you? Apparently you and I have had a violent row and you never want to work with me again, and I want to know what it's all about.'

❝So he said, 'Well, I'm leaving the band', by which time he had already met Ronnie Dio out here and made his mind up. So I said, if that's what you really want to do, you go ahead and do it, but I'm not going to pack it in. Then he works it round that he forced me out so he could do what he really wanted to do – because the name Black Sabbath is a hard name to follow.**❞** 1979

❝In the end, Tony and I didn't talk any more. It was all a bit sad and a really depressing end to the band. But there's no bitterness now. They've got their band and I hope they do really well and I've got my band and I know we're going to do the best we can.
The best of luck to all of us.❞

1980

❝In Sabbath I was only singing another riff to Tony Iommi's riff and, well people'd think you were mad if you went to work whistling 'Iron Man'. The last two or three albums with Sabbath I didn't enjoy, the last one I hated. Now I've got the freedom to combine power with melody – give them something to remember.**❞** 1981

OUT OF THE DARKNESS

"I wasn't really happy with Sabbath and the way things were going over the last two or three albums before I left. I mean, it was really getting away from everything Sabbath had been based on in the first place. What we needed was a good, strong producer who could direct us in the studio and someone who wasn't too directly involved in the band personally. Instead we were trying to produce ourselves and getting lost...

"Tony was always trying to make the band more sophisticated. I mean there was one time when he brought in a load of string players on a session. I walked into the studio and there were all these guys of about 50 sitting around waiting for their go. I thought to myself, 'What the hell is all this?' I mean – violinists on a Black Sabbath album! If I'd been a fan, I wouldn't have believed it.

"On stage Tony used to go into these great long guitar solos which were like jazz. I mean, jazz at a Black Sabbath gig – ridiculous. I used to watch him from the side of the stage and cringe when Tony did that sort of thing. I used to hide. I'm not knocking him technically because I still think he's a really brilliant guitar player. But his jazz solos used to slow things down." 1981

"I wanted to get back to good basic hard rock, like we were known for. I wouldn't have minded doing the new stuff if it was reproduceable on stage, but it wasn't. Fucking hell, it took so long to do. It was done in three sections and joined together. No way could you do that onstage. They'd think you were R2D2! Studios drive me up the wall. After a month or two in one of those places I feel like a bat.

"Fuck this overdubbing and all that mechanical crap, Tony Iommi playing through a jar of Vaseline or something. On the last album, on that track 'Break Out', I couldn't believe it one Sunday morning when 30 guys with trumpets marched in and started playing on a Black Sabbath album. It nearly made my hair fall out!" (1979)

"They'll [Sabbath without Ozzy] probably sound very much like Foreigner – that was the last album they were into!" 1979

TONY IOMMI AND RONNIE DIO **OUT OF THE DARKNESS**

"... towards the end of Sabbath it was very depressing. It was a real bad mess and that's the strongest memory I have – Black Sabbath was as black as its name at the end of the day."

"Sabbath falling apart was a natural thing. The fun had gone, like a marriage, y'know. You look at your wife one day and suddenly think, 'I don't love you anymore.' The best years with Sabbath were up to *Sabbath Bloody Sabbath*, and after that we started to deteriorate. We were all totally fucked up on drugs and alcohol, in a terrible state with cocaine and booze and fucking uppers and downers and this and that and pot, and whatever, and we just forgot how to do it together." 1990

"It's like a divorce, you say, 'You take the couch, I'll take the sideboard', then as time goes along, the partner wants the couch *and* the sideboard. What I can't understand about Los Angeles is, you'll get somebody divorcing his wife, I'll divorce my wife, he'll marry my wife, I'll marry his wife and we'll all still go out to fucking dinner. Well, in reality it don't work out! Of course I wanted to be the best, and they wanted to do better, you start saying bad things..." **1997**

"Anyway we came to a crossroads in the band. I was uncomfortable and I really couldn't decide whether to go or to stay. Whatever I suggested the band didn't like. No-one listened to me at all and it was a real drag. You've got no idea how that feels. You can't keep going in a situation like that. Anyway we decided to pack it in – the whole band. We were going to do a farewell tour and that would be the end of it. The band would split up and the name wouldn't be used by any members.
"The farewell tour never happened and the band met up with Ronnie before I went to Los Angeles to see about my band. They just got him in and carried on as Sabbath. I'm not bitter about that, but honestly I was surprised because I thought everything had been decided as far as farewell tours and all that was concerned." 1980

“Ronnie Dio's an alright guy. I've got nothing against him particularly. But the thing is, I'd never consider joining Rainbow and singing Ronnie Dio songs and to my mind he should never have joined Black Sabbath and started to sing my songs. There's no integrity doing that. In a band, you can replace a guitarist, a bassist or a drummer easily enough, but a vocalist's practically indispensable.

“What would happen if you took Mick Jagger out of The Rolling Stones and put, say, Freddie Mercury in the group instead? It'd be a disaster. I don't mind Dio teaming up with Iommi, but I can never forgive him for singing my songs and for them choosing to continue to play under the name Black Sabbath. It's a con.” 1980

“I wasn't just depressed, I was suicidal. I stayed in a hotel room in Hollywood for six months and never opened the drapes. I lived like a slob.” 1998, ON HIS DEPARTURE FROM THE BAND

“… it's only after I left Sabbath that I realised how great an influence it was.”

OUT OF THE DARKNESS

Solo Flight

THE SOLO YEARS FROM 1981 ON

❝I'd been trying to get my own band together long before I officially left Sabbath. I was in Los Angeles. I was there working in a studio with Gary Moore and Glenn Hughes also got involved. Glenn didn't last very long with us, but Gary was a phenomenal player. He's really, genuinely brilliant. He would have been great to work with but he wanted to get his own band together.

❝I don't think our ideas were really the same and both of us really wanted to be boss. To be honest, Gary was a bit too good for me. My whole idea was to get to basics in any band that I was getting together. I needed hard-driving, really *heavy* music, straightforward stuff that kids could get into.❞ 1981

❝I never thought I'd be able to do it on my own, get my own band together. I thought I was fucked, ruined, finished. I was in such a mental state when I left Sabbath I was screwed up in every possible way. Life hadn't been good for a long time in that band, it really *had* become Black Sabbath, everything was dark, gloomy and depressing. It was very sordid and sticky. I wasn't into their music and they weren't into mine.

❝The rest of the guys in Sabbath became boring old farts if you like, and there I was, this crazy guy, still into wrecking hotel rooms, and having parties. It just didn't work. I mean, how can you go up onstage and shout 'Yeah I love you all! Rock'n'roll forever!' and then go to bed at 10 o'clock with a nightcap on, a candle in your hand and a bible under your arm. But that was what the others were into!" 1980

"It's not definite that we'll call it Son of Sabbath yet. I might get some of those lunatic Son of Sam people in New York chasing me up. Rock Star Gets Shot. It's still copping out on the Sabbath name really though, isn't it? And Sabbath's dead now as far as I'm concerned. I might just call it Ozzy." 1979

"This is a new band I have now, and it's fresh and we're working very hard. Forget all this Rolls-Royce limousine garbage. The only thing to do is just get on a bus like anybody else, have fun and be real. It's back to basics again." 1980

"I'm as happy as a pig in shit at the moment. Couldn't be happier. I don't really think about Sabbath any more. I've no hard feelings, they can just get up and get on with it. I don't care what they do." 1980

"The big problem was trying to get a drummer. I tried to get one through auditions and it was really murder. It was so embarrassing. There was this one guy who was *huge*. He came in with these enormous boots on and said, 'Hey, it's the man' to me.

SOLO FLIGHT

He kept on saying that. He was mad, I think. He wasn't too good either. That was just as well really because looking at the size of his boots you knew his hamburger bill would have been about a hundred dollars a day and that would have broken me in about a month.**"** 1980

"We'd tried to manage ourselves and it had been a disaster and I was always on about getting a manager to take the weight off us. When we went with Don (Arden) I was really pleased. He had big plans for us, and for the first time in years I really felt confident that things were going to go well for Black Sabbath. But when I left I was really down. I thought I was going right down the tubes. I kept on thinking what's going to happen to me now? And it was a real surprise what happened.

"Don let Sabbath go and kept me on. He just came to me and said, 'If you still want a manager for yourself, then that's great because I want to do it.' He gave me all the encouragement I needed and he gave me a lot of confidence in myself. If it hadn't been for Don and Jet Records I don't know what would have happened. They helped me a lot when I decided to go out and start forming my band. The whole thing's like a family and, despite what you hear about Don, I've still got both my arms and both my legs!**"** **1980, ON MANAGER AND FUTURE FATHER-IN-LAW DON ARDEN**

"(Bassist) Bob Daisley was the meanest, tightest bastard I've ever met. He's got short arms and long pockets. (Drummer) Lee (Kerslake)'s lovely and I've got no bad things to say about him. I hope he's still a friend. But it just wasn't working for me. And anyway I've always wanted Tommy (Aldridge) right from the start. Y'know how you have that dream of building the ultimate band? Tommy was with Pat Travers when I was first forming the band, but when he was free I just had to have him."

1981, ON CHANGING THE LINE-UP OF THE BAND

"I didn't like working with Sabbath for the last four or five years, so what I do now is change the band when it gets dodgy – that keeps it fresh and alive... my favourite line-up is the one I have now. The last one was terrible – Phil Soussan was a fucking terrible bass player, and Jake E Lee was the miserablist man God ever bred. There was only me and Randy Castillo, who's still with me now."

"If you can laugh at your mistakes, then you're gonna be over the moon at your good things – but if you're living with a miserable fucker who never speaks to you, it spreads through the band like a cancer. When you did a good gig with Jake, you thought you were going to fucking hang yourself." 1990

"You need young guys – why should I want old farts around me? I'm old enough. But having young guys in the band keeps me young, it keeps me in touch with what the kids are about. I was reading about Mick Jagger: Jagger doesn't employ anyone older than 30 in his organisation. I really think that's the only way to keep up with the younger generation!"

"I'm 36 years of age but I don't feel it. I just get on with the job. I'd much rather have young musicians with me than when you look to the back of the stage and see all those bald patches. It's like the old Whitesnake band: great musicians, but they looked like an old blues band. And the older generation don't buy the records like the younger kids do." 1985

"Well, Jake and I just parted company. Musically for the last 12 months we had not been hitting it off. He lost interest in me and

SOLO FLIGHT

OZZY *Talking*

I kinda lost interest in him. He grew out of me, but I kept putting off the task of finding another bloody guitar player. I thought there wouldn't be any good ones, but do you know what? There's a *million* out there! But you can imagine how many crackpots come along as well. A third of them are legitimate, a third know what they're doing... and a third are fucking fruitcakes who want to meet me.

"I just let it be known I was looking for a guitarist and word of mouth does a faster job than radio or TV... I wasn't looking for a guy who can play great, just a guy I can live with offstage and work and write with. I don't want a speed freak. This Speed Metal business, it's like a runaway train. That kind of music does my head in!" 1986, ON FINDING A REPLACEMENT FOR AXEMAN JAKE E LEE

"For the first month it's very hard for new guys because they all believe what they've read in the papers. They think I'm a lunatic with an axe who runs around chopping people's heads off all day. I'm not like that at all!" 1986

"As far as me and Zakk (Wylde) are concerned, is that I'm proud to have discovered a new talent. The most rewarding thing is remembering this raggedy-arsed kid walking through the door and ultimately becoming this great guy. And Zakk Wylde is a great fuckin' guy! The whole band is. I've worked with quite a few arseholes over the years, but these guys are great to work with."

1994

"Zakk's everything I've been looking for: he's got a great personality, he's dedicated to his instrument and he's just wonderful to have around 'cos he's always up – he's never down. In rehearsals and that he'll tell me off sometimes and make me do things which is just great – he's so different to Jake who never said anything to anybody. I never knew what he was doing, y'know? We all communicate, like a family and Zakk's only 21, he's brilliant and, let's face it, he'll only get better." 1989

"I've met Steve Vai a couple of times and he seems like a very nice guy." FEBRUARY 1994

OZZY AND ZAKK WYLDE

❝I was working with Steve Vai earlier in the year, and while Steve never treated me like anything less than a gentleman and I was fine with him, it was felt that maybe I should work with actual songwriters.❞ DECEMBER 1994

❝I haven't had a bad run with guitarists. It's gone well with everybody except Jake E Lee – and I don't know what the fuck happened to him.**❞ 1994**

❝I don't write songs by myself, I don't play an instrument. I don't know what fucking key I'm singing in. I don't know one end of the guitar from the other. So I go from instinct: if the hair on my arms is standing up, and I get a tickling feeling up my back, I go, 'That's a good song!" 2001

❝I don't like talking about my lyrics because it sounds like you're trying to make an excuse for what you've written. As an artist I should be free to write about anything I want, but people read things into everything. That's how I end up in trouble. I've never told anyone to kill themselves in a song but I still got blamed when that kid blew his head off.**❞ 1998**

The Late, Great Randy Rhoads

"When he turned up, unfortunately, I was stoned out of my mind – I mean, I was on another planet. Some guy woke me up and said, 'He's here.' I looked up and Randy started playing from this tiny amp. Even in my semi-consciousness he blew my mind. I told him to come by the next day and that he had the gig." 1998

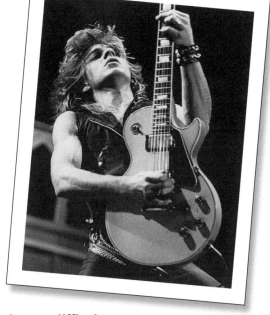

"Randy was the first guy that ever gave me time. I have a lot of ideas in my head, but being as how I don't play an instrument, to put them across musically is very difficult for me. Randy had the patience and the time to hear me out and work ideas out with me, which relieved me of such a great frustration that I'd built up over the years with Sabbath, because they never gave me the time of day to put my things forward.

"Randy was a truly wonderful guy, and I'm not just saying that because he's dead. I think, had he lived he'd have blown the balls off Eddie Van Halen by now." 1990

"I just sort of bumped into him and he turned out to be phenomenal. The only thing is, he's incredibly thin. So's his girlfriend. When the two of them make love it must be like a couple of sticks rubbing together." 1980

"When we were recording, he would disappear in the studio for days. I'd ask him what he was doing and he would say, 'I'm working on this solo and I still can't get it.' Finally it would come to him and he would call me and say, 'Listen to this.' It would always tear my head off." 1998

SOLO FLIGHT

"At approximately 9am on Friday 19 March 1982, I was awoken from my sleep by a loud explosion. I immediately thought we'd hit a vehicle on the road. I got out of bed screaming to my fiancée, Sharon, 'Get off the bus!' After getting out of the bus, I saw that a plane had crashed. I didn't know who was on the plane at the time. When we realised that our people were on the plane, I found it very difficult to get assistance from anyone to help. In fact, it took almost a half-hour before anyone arrived.

"One small fire engine arrived which appeared to squirt three gallons of water over the inferno. We asked for further assistance, such as telephones, and didn't receive any further help. In the end, we finally found a telephone and Sharon phoned her father."

SWORN AFFIDAVIT TO US AUTHORITIES FOLLOWING THE ACCIDENT

"In the few short years before Randy died, I had gone through so much. My father had died, I got kicked out of Sabbath – I was up and down, up and down. Then Randy got killed. At that point I said to Sharon, 'I can't keep doing this', and she said, 'Yes you can. If Randy was alive, this is what he'd want you to do.' So I decided the best thing to do was to get back out on the road. And it wasn't the most amazing show, but we did it." 1998

"I suppose the same thing's going to happen to me one day. The price you pay I suppose. The death rate in rock'n'roll is phenomenal. You live at 100 miles per hour, 24 hours a day. And your body can only take so much." 1981

"You know, you always think 'Oh, poor Randy', and he was really close to his mother... and now I've got children of my own, I'd be devastated if I was to lose one. She must've been devastated. When I read that letter, it cracked me up: I couldn't finish reading it 'cos I've been trying to avoid looking at it square-on for all these years. It's like I've tried to avoid it in whatever way I could... It affected me, reading that letter, more than the whole thing because I've been trying to dodge it; I've spoken about it but I must've stuffed so much grief down, I just cracked up, broke down.

"I don't know if you've ever lost anyone close to you, but it's kind of like your body switches off a certain pain. Jesus Christ it's been five years and it's gone in a flash." 1987

"The fondest memory of Randy Rhoads is just him. He was an incredible talent. Whereas you might say of great guitar players that their instruments are extensions of them, with Randy it was the other way around. He was an extension of his instrument. On every off day, he'd get a classical guitar teacher to give him a lesson.

"When I first met him, I thought he was gay, he looked so effeminate. He used to wear high-heeled shoes, because he was so short. He was a lot of fun. If ever I could say I was in love with another man, I was in love with his spirit. I mean, not in a physical sense. But he was beyond a friend to me.**"** 2001

"Randy Rhoads will always remind me of a time in my life and career when things took off again."

SECOND *BLIZZARD OF OZZ* LINE-UP...
(L-R) RUDY SARZO, DON AIREY, OZZY, RANDY RHOADS, TOMMY ALDRIDGE

SOLO FLIGHT

Ozzy: The Music

HIS POST-SABBATH OUTPUT

Blizzard Of Ozz

❝One thing's for sure, there aren't any ballads. It's all strong stuff.❞

1980

❝All the songs we've written ourselves and we had them all ready before we went into the studio. That made a nice change from a lot of recording with Sabbath. We used to go in with about two songs written and do the rest in the studio. That was crazy, really, because it ended up costing us a fortune in studio time when we should have actually been recording... as far as this band is concerned, we all work together on writing songs and we discuss how we're going to do them.❞ 1980

'Suicide Solution'

❝You do know that he (Bon Scott of AC/DC) died – he choked on his own vomit – and I was into the same sort of thing for a while, drinking to excess. That song is a warning. I don't want it to happen to me.❞

Diary Of A Madman

"The first LP was good, but too much of it was a reflection of what was going through my head about Sabbath. This is much more like what I sound like – and when I record with the new band, well, there'll be no comparison.**"** 1981

"I just released my new album *Diary Of A Madman* which has been an idea of mine for the last five years. I am happy with the success of my debut *Blizzard Of Ozz* album and the tens of thousands of followers that have come out to see the shows... but I think something has changed me. I keep seeing visions of my birth, my life and my death. I have become infatuated with the feeling of horror.

"My fascination with life's phobias have manifested themselves on this new record. I only hope its tracks will freeze the blood and make the flesh creep to make people understand that this is Ozzy music. If my ideas seem disordered in intellect or slightly psychotic... it is because they are. I am Ozzy Osbourne." 1981

"We're also making a movie of *Diary Of A Madman*, it'll be like an underground movie, a lot like the truth – not all the phoney glamour side of rock. I hate all that posing. Why can't people just be people and throw up now and again. We all crap, even the Queen... but at least, Lady Di's stopped phoning me up now!**"** 1981

OZZY: THE MUSIC ,,

Talk Of The Devil
Double Live Album

❝Here's some songs I used to do with Black Sabbath before they employed a midget. How can a four-foot poof sing about the Devil?❞

❝I'm really happy with the way it's turned out. It's got 'Children Of The Grave', 'Paranoid', 'Iron Man', 'The Wizard', 'NIB', 'Snowblind', 'Sweet Leaf', 'Fairies Wear Boots' and a couple more. But we've done 1980s versions of them – we haven't stuck to the book, we've updated them all.❞ 1982

Bark At The Moon

❝... the songs were pretty good, but the mixing was a rushed job. You can record for months and months but it's all down to the final mix, you know? There were a couple of songs on that album with real bad mixes, like 'Waiting For The Darkness'...❞ **1986**

The Ultimate Sin

"There's some regular headbanging shit: 'Killer Of Giants' is a really heavy sound, like an early Sabbath thing. And there's one song called 'Thank God For The Bomb' which should cause some outrage... but it's funny, you can take it either way. If we didn't have the bomb, everybody'd be killing each other with regular guns. At least it's a deterrent. CND? Fuck 'em! I'll have the anti-nuclear squad, the RSPCA, the God squad, all after me.

"And there's no ballads, not after the last one. I mean, you're bound to get a cross-section audience and in the end, you have to make up your own mind what you're about. I'm not gonna jump for a name producer. I don't care who does it as long as I can sit down at the end of the day and be pleased with the result." **1985**

"(Producer) Ron Nevison is working out just fucking great. He doesn't try and push things too far. He really encourages you to let rip – whether the vocals end up sounding flat or whatever, he doesn't seem to care for these early sessions – Ron just wants us all to really give this thing everything we've got. And to get it, he's prepared to let us have our own heads in the studio. It's great because every album I've done since leaving Sabbath has always seemed so fucking rushed." 1985

"To be honest with you, although there were good songs on that album and we spent a lot of time doing them, working with a producer like Ron Nevison wasn't a very enjoyable task for me. He changed the whole colour of the album from the way I thought it was going to sound. It was like being in the Boy Scouts..." **1986**

"It was the biggest chart album I've ever had. But when I think of it I remember a very sterile environment – I don't have fond memories of that project." 1986

OZZY: THE MUSIC

Tribute
(Dedicated To Randy Rhoads)

"I said to Sharon, you can put it out but please make it interesting – don't put it out at some ludicrous price and with a black album cover showing a guitar leaning against a tombstone. You know the one thing I've always tried to do is give value for money." 1987

"Randy Rhoads was a lovely guy, and I think that the *Tribute* album is a beautiful memory of him."

No Rest For The Wicked

"I've taken it right back to the original heaviness. The songs on *The Ultimate Sin* were okay, but the production was too tame, too Americanised – a lot of people disagree and say that it was the best record I ever made, but, well, I have to like it. I don't really care what people write about me any more, if I did I'd never make another record, so if I like the record they can say what the hell they like about it. My preference matters, and if I prefer this album to the last one then so what? I never said anything else about *The Ultimate Sin* – I never pretended it was my favourite." 1989

"I think that this LP, more than any, has the root of Sabbath in it. And of course I think this album's great. I had fun making it, I really did. Just as I'm having the greatest fun in ages touring."

"I did this album with Roy Thomas Baker and took it home to listen to, cause in the studio after a while you don't know what the fuck you're hearing. So when Keith Olsen got it to mix, he told me I didn't have a 72-piece band so I didn't need a 72-track album. He stripped the tapes right down."

Ozzmosis

X-Ray was the working title of the album when I was working with
Steve Vai, so I don't really wanna call it anything right now... I still
feel I'm two good ol' Ozzy rockers short of a great selection. But in
my whole career I've never had as many good songs written in my
life! I've got enough for a couple of albums at the moment.**"** 1994

**"I've always worked in a band environment where we just jam
through stuff and work things out as we go. Previously the band
would spend the first two hours talking about what they were up
to last night, how many chicks they got a blow-job off, how
many beers they'd drunk, how many titty bars they'd been to...
working with real songwriters is a whole learning process for
both parties.**
**"I was first paired with Mark Hudson and Steve Dudas and I was
amazed at how quickly it was coming out. But it's because these
guys are professional fucking
songwriters. I've had a lot of
fun with them on the way,
too – and while I won't be
using all the stuff we wrote,
I'll be keeping a good part
of it. Then came the Jim
Vallance thing. I think Jim
and I learned a lot off each
other."** 1994

"I don't like things to
sound absolutely perfect.
I like to hear a few
mistakes, fingers sliding up
guitar strings, some clicks
and bumps. Bollocks to
those ultra-perfect-
sounding albums.**"** 1994

"At this stage of the game, the only thing I can pick up on is that this is going to be a very heavy fucking album! No more 'Goodbye To Romance' or 'Mama I'm Comin' Home' – that's all fuckin' dead and history man!"

"I thought I was gettin' out of the darkness when 'Mama...' was a hit, but no. Every time I try to get out of the darkness, it drags me back. But I'm very optimistic about how it will turn out, because Michael (Beinhorn) is a good producer and ultimately we're working very very hard... there's no turning back now... I've lived with these songs for a long time. And if you think I'm bad now, wait until the mix, wait until the mastering! I'll wanna kill everybody! Because for the rest of my life it's me who'll live with this record!" 1995

Just Say Ozzy (Live)

"When my record company came up with this idea my first thought was 'Oh no, not another version of old Sabbath songs with a couple of mine thrown in'. But when I started to listen to all the shows we played on the last tour, my thoughts changed. I'm happier with this version of 'Shot In The Dark' than the originals. And the Sabbath songs – to have recorded them one last time says it all for me. It's a chapter of my musical career I can now close."

Down To Earth

"I had a very, very bad time on the last album with Michael Beinhorn, So I felt kind of gun-shy about producers; I wanted to produce it myself, but I haven't got a fucking clue." 2001

"If I'm gonna pay someone a million dollars to make a record with me than I better like how we work. Last time out it turned out that I paid a guy a million dollars to abuse me. Why would I wanna get back into that situation in a hurry?" 2001

❝I say to all my guitar players, 'I want you to play a riff that will make a kid out there want to be the next Jimmy Page. Don't sound like fucking Steve Howe from Yes, or do all that finger tapping like Eddie Van Halen!'❞ **2001**

❝**I didn't want an Ozzy Osbourne All-Star album, where you need a book to keep track of who's playing; that never worked for me. So no matter who wrote the songs, Zakk was the guitar player at the end of the day. It just came down to chemistry.**❞ 2001

❝I like to make a piece of work, rather than have one track sound like the next, and I always put a couple of mellow songs on there. There's this really good variety on this album ('Down To Earth'), and Zakk's playing is fucking awesome.❞ **2001**

❝**Because of the amount of time that's lapsed between** *Ozzmosis* **and now, when I started this album, I thought, 'where the fuck do I fit into today's world? Where does Ozzy Osbourne fit?' I mean, I can't do this rap shit, or these big Satan growling voices; that's just not my thing.**❞ 2001

❝The reason why I'm calling it *Down To Earth* is the album cover. What the guy did was X-ray my whole body, and then take photographs of my whole body. Then he put the X-ray under the picture of my skin, so it looks like a skeleton with jewellery on, and tattoos. I'm looking at this and thinking, 'What the fuck am I going to call this thing?' Then I was sitting in my hotel room thinking, 'Let's go right back to the beginning. What got you to this point? The first name of Black Sabbath was Earth,' and I went, 'Bingo! That's it! It's all down to Earth that I came here, and this looks like an alien coming down to earth.'❞ **2001**

Suicide & Censorship

OZZY, AMERICA & THE MORAL MAJORITY

"... this kid who committed suicide, it was never my intention to write a song so a kid would put a fucking gun to his head! I copped the fucking blame." 1989

"Naturally I've got lawyers defending me, but I don't really know how far it's got. I try not to let it enter my everyday life 'cos I can't take responsibility for it – causing their deaths was not my intention, y'know? If they think so then I feel sorry for them too. You've got to try and ignore it because around each corner there lurks another writ. I mean, Judas Priest have just been served one but Ozzy's always the target, I think they believe that if they topple me then everything will go away. "What makes it even more annoying is that it's often done with the ulterior motive such as a husband who's running for President, etc, and they want to get as much publicity for their campaign. I feel sorry for Priest 'cos I know the suicides weren't their intention, but what's

ROB HALFORD OF JUDAS PRIEST

the difference between records and horror films? It's all entertainment, yet film directors aren't held responsible for deaths like we are – it's just so annoying.** 1989

"When I go to America, it's not me you have to worry about, it's all of them – the PMRC who try to ban the shows and the fuckin' sheriff in Texas who says he can't guarantee my safety if I show my face in town. These are the people that cause all the trouble in America. I don't have to lift a finger.**"**

"I tell ya, I could release a version of 'My Way' and somebody in America would find something to read into it, something disgusting. You know on the beginning of 'Blood Bath In Paradise' from the new album – all those weird noises and that weird talking? That's all a big joke. If you play it backwards it says. 'Your mother sells whelks in Hull'. I'm still waiting for some dickhead to pick up on that and tell people I'm sending messages to the Devil."

"There must be some sick people working for these censorship boards. They must be a bunch of perverts to read anything into that 'Crazy Babies' video. It makes me sick. I mean if I had a pair of tits and my name was Madonna, they wouldn't have blinked an eye.**"**

"America is getting heavy. Anything sensational they just go for it. I'm desperately frightened that some guy's going to blow me away. Some of these guys are nuts. They want to take it too far. All it is you know, I'm a clown. A terrible old showbiz ham. I'm not a musician. I'm not a singer. So why do they take it all so seriously? I just get people off. I'm their joint if you like. They smoke me and they get high." 1981

"I can't even fart without someone saying it caused their cat to jump on a fire. I did this controversial chat show in America and they were saying my music causes kids to fucking go satanic and all this crap. In America, one of the craziest nights of the year is Halloween when they all dress up as fucking gooks and freaks and monsters and whatever. Yet when I do it every night of the week on stage, they term me a fucking anti-Christ. Take that Madonna video with those burning crosses. I'd have my arse nailed to a fucking cross if I did that." 1990

"I listen to my audience, not the bullshit that gets spoken in the clubs on Sunset Boulevard or in the press. I respect people's time and people's opinions but at the end of the day, get off my fucking back, y'know?" 2001

"If Bill Clinton can't get a blow job off his secretary then he's in the wrong job." 1998

"I spend more time in America, but it's only while my kids go to school. As soon as they're done, I'm out of here like a bat out of hell. The weather's nice in LA, but you can't beat a good plate of fish and chips." 2000

Animal Instinct

BATS, DOVES & THE ALAMO

The Bat Incident

"I thought it was a plastic toy so I just grabbed this thing , bit the head off and thought 'Fuck me! It was flapping...'**"** 1997

"I put it in my mouth and spat it straight out. Not very nice – all crunchy and warm!" 1988

"... some people look at me and they expect me to walk around with a fucking bag full of bats! 'Hi there, wanna bat?' It's not real, you know? It's called entertainment.**"**

"Snakes, dead mice, rats and the bat. That happened in Des Moines, Iowa. You can't imagine how many times I've been asked about that fucking bat."

1990

OZZY *Talking*

Biting The Head Off A Dove

❝I've been in this business 15 years and if they realised the shit I have to go through for my name to be remembered... I was at a CBS convention. You don't realise what these business things are like. All the old codgers are there and they don't give a fuck about you, it's just a sham. They play your album while you're there and then forget you. Well I wanted to make a real impression.

❝The scam is the bird was dead. We were planning to release it there but it died beforehand. So rather than waste it I bit its head off. You should have seen their faces. They all went white. They were speechless. That girl in the pictures was screaming. Eventually a bloke came up and said, 'You better go'. It tasted warm, like tomato sauce. Next time it'll be a piranha fish.❞ **1981**

❝**People have gone on and on about that fucking bird – it's over six months ago now. Why make a big deal about it? There's people going hungry – at least I had food. Everyone's selling their pigeons round where I live just in case. I'm gonna start on parrots next – at least they can say "No, no" as me teeth close in!❞** 1981

❝It tasted like a good hamburger.❞ **1988**

❝**I was well pissed, man, well pissed.❞** 1989

The Aftermath...

"I said bring your own offal to the gig instead of having a custard pie fight. We was going to throw the meat at each other. Fuck me, man. Talk about a snowball sliding down the edge, um, down a mountain turning into an avalanche. It was insane, fucking hell man, insane! I was gettin' fucking chicken legs, fucking dead cats, it was fucking unbelievable.

"One night a cop came back stage and says to me, 'Do you realise the effect you're having on these kids?' I said, 'It's just a bit of fun, what's the matter with ya?' He showed me a photo of a kid waiting outside to go into the concert with a cow's head on his shoulder!"

1989

"One night someone threw this fucking swamp frog and I swear it was the size of a baby – it landed on its back, and it even looked like a little baby." 1990

"What's the difference between a dove and a chicken anyway? One poxy bird. They wanna see me when I start on cats. I shot a cat once for shitting on my car. The cat cost 35p and the car cost six grand – no contest." 1981

"I'd like to learn to juggle cats onstage – see how that went down. The other day we were somewhere where they had a moat thing round a castle, with sharks in it. And there was this cat asleep on the wall. I elbowed it – and I tell you that cat didn't even touch the water. They say Christ walked on water – but I saw a cat do it!" 1981

"Oh no, I've never shot a cat! I once shot a horse. It's just that I dig shooting. I've got guns in the house." 1982

"I used to work with horses, I used to strangle them."

"I hunt rabbits and pheasant and milkmen, delivery men, taxmen, neighbours..." 1978

ANIMAL INSTINCT

❝I went outside dressed in just my underpants and wellied them (his wife's chickens) with a shotgun. Then I stabbed one with a fucking great big sword. I was covered in feathers, blood and chicken shit. The nice lady from next door peered over the fence and said, 'Ah, John, I see you're back. Unwinding'❞ 1998

❝Animal rights campaigners are all hypocrites. Anyone who complains, just ask the arseholes do they eat meat, and if they do they're worse than me 'cos they're lazy bastards. They're so dumb they believe in the system, they believe it's all right to go to the butcher's and see a dead cow hanging up as long as they don't have to kill it. Y'know what I'd like to do? I'd like to open up a restaurant and every time someone ordered a steak I'd bring a live cow in and slaughter it in front of them. Every time people eat meat, they should think of me – I'm a great advert for the vegetarian society.❞ **1981**

❝I had this wild dream in America. I was looking at all these people in a restaurant eating their steaks and talking about their cars and yachts and houses. I thought it would be great to get a cow, stand it in the restaurant and the next time someone ordered a steak just hack a lump off it and throw it on the table. They'd keep on talking about their yachts. They'd be too involved and too polite to say anything.❞ 1976

❝On the *Diary Of A Madman* tour (1982), kids were bringing raw meat, dead cats, dead dogs, anything they could get their hands on. I was backstage in the States before one show and this cop marched in and handed me a Polaroid that had just been taken outside. He's like, 'Which one of you is Ozzy Bourne?' He couldn't even get my fucking name right – and there's a picture of this guy in line with a horse's head... he's killed a fucking horse on the way to the gig. I started laughing, but the cop didn't see the funny side.❞ **1998**

❝I believe it was meant to happen. But I don't relish it on my tombstone. It'll be: Ozzy Osbourne, the man who bit the head off a bat... I mean, it's so long ago, man.❞ 2001

"I've got a Chihuahua, a Pomeranian, a Japanese Chin, a British Bulldog, another Chihuahua, another Japanese Chin, a German shepherd, a boxer and a bull mastiff... They all taste the same." 2001

Urinating On The Alamo & Other Outrages

"Everyone's got it wrong. I didn't get arrested for pissing on the Alamo. I got arrested for being pissed at the Alamo. The Yanks don't understand English slang. I told them I got pissed at the Alamo and it came out that I pissed all over everywhere. I said I was gonna get pissed at the White House too and I got the FBI classifying me as a national security threat. If you tell a Yank you want a packet of fags the silly bastard'll bring you 20 homosexuals. I can't play Texas at all because of it." 1982

"A genuine mistake." 1988

ANIMAL INSTINCT ,,

"I've had more front covers for pissing over the Alamo than I did for selling two million albums. It's like I became a professional practical joker rather than the professional entertainer and musician. I once read a thing about Keith Moon and he said, 'If I was to sit in a bar drinking Perrier water and acting normal, someone is bound to come up to me and say, "Are you okay?", 'cos if you're not screaming round the bar with your dick out they think something is wrong with you!'

"The latest one I heard about me is I've just come from New York where I was allegedly mugged. I've been shot four times and propelled a bullet away with the back of me hand! Listen, if someone pulled a knife on me, you'd hear this big farting noise, followed by a big smell, and I'd be running. There'd be a big steaming pile of brown stuff on the floor..." **1987**

"**Every interview I ever did in my own solo career, without fail, there would be The Three Questions: 'Did you bite the head off a bat?', 'Did you piss up the Alamo?', and 'Are Black Sabbath getting back together again?' I could do the fucking interview in my sleep! 'Yes', 'Yes' and 'No!'**" 1997

"I was taking drugs so much I was a wreck. The final straw came when I shot all (his and first wife Thelma's) cats. We had about 17, and I went crazy and shot them all. My wife found me under the piano in a white suit, a shotgun in one hand and a knife in the other." **1998**

"**I don't remember anything – I was *gone*! I went to court and everything, but she dropped the charges. All that craziness stopped once I put the cork back into the bottle.**"

ON ATTACKING HIS WIFE SHARON

"I'm supposed to be the madman of rock'n'roll. Well if I'm supposed to be this nutter I don't mind. I'd rather be in the Ozzy Osbourne Band than The Pet Shop Boys, that's for sure. I ain't wimpy. I'm not fake. I just do whatever I want."

"I'm very shy, always have been. I don't like cameras at all and I fucking hate making videos. I never watch myself on TV either. I think my Birmingham accent makes me sound like a moron."

1997

"I never think of myself as being cool. I don't try to be cool... I've seen some real cool fucking idiots make complete twats of themselves. I've seen many a rock star fall down loads of fucking stairs because they had sunglasses on indoors and they couldn't see a bloody thing. Then again, I've made a complete prick of myself so many times. But I got away with it, because I was Ozzy Osbourne and that gave me a license to be an asshole." 1997

"When I get drunk I end up saying the stupidest fucking things – I read the paper and I think why the fuck did I say that? You don't want to sit here talking to a drunken fucking slob 'cos I'm going to look a dickhead when the interview comes out..." 1989

"I feel stereotyped in the same way as Christopher Reeve, the guy who played Superman. He may be a great actor, but whatever he does I expect him to take his shirt off and reveal a big "S" on his chest!" 1995

"I mean, someone asked me, 'What's Stevie like?' and I said, 'Stevie who? Oh, hang on, what's she do?' and they said, 'Stevie Nicks out of Fleetwood Mac' and I thought, 'Oh yes?' and they said, 'Well, didn't you run away with her?' And like I've never met Stevie Nicks in my fucking life! The minds that think these things up must be *incredible*." 1987

"I'm scared to death of this AIDS thing. I won't even share a cigarette with anybody. If somehow I got it, it wouldn't matter, I'd have to deal with it – I'd be terrified of passing it to my wife or kids... My dad used to say that a standing cock hasn't got a conscience and if you've got a belly full of booze you won't give a fuck. If you're pissed and you've got a porker you're unlikely to say, 'Hold on love, give me half an hour to nip to the chemists and buy a rubber!'"

ANIMAL INSTINCT

Ultimate Sins

OZZY'S ADDICTIONS & HOW HE BEAT THEM

❝I believe I'm going nuts. But so what? As long as I'm enjoying it!❞

1972

❝**I shook myself out of all that pop-star crap. If I'd carried on with all the boozing and what have you, I'd have burnt myself out by now.**❞ 1976

❝I get high. I get fucked up. What the hell's wrong with getting fucked up? There must be something wrong with the system if so many people have to get fucked up. Too much of anything will kill you in the end. Cigarettes are the worst. Petrol fumes will kill you, rocket fuel will kill you. The planet will kill you in the end... I never take dope or anything before I go onstage. I'll smoke a joint or whatever afterwards. But I'm not into drugs; I don't believe in it any more. I think it's false, you're living a lie when you have to take that all the time.❞ **1978**

❝**I have this little demon that keeps making me drink. I just love drinking and getting drunk. I'll drink anything. If it takes my fancy, I'll drink it. I'm the Dean Martin of heavy metal, I am. I'm not as mad as everyone makes out... I'm worse. I go mad on booze. I smash things up and set fire to myself. I set fire to my sleeve the other night when I fell in the fire drunk. I drink Perrier**

OZZY Talking

water to cut my intake down, I don't want to be another rock'n'roll suicide. I laid off the booze totally for three or four weeks. I'd go into pubs surrounded by people full of beer and think 'Was I as bad as that?' When I'm not at work, I get bored and start drinking.**"** 1980

"You name it, I drank it, from whisky to gin and cider. I didn't care if I lived or died.**" 1989**

"Everyone blames rock'n'roll for their problems. But let me tell you the truth. It's a great way to make a living. But if you want to be an idiot and take bags of drugs and drink, you will die. I've tried the lot and I'm not proud of it." 1989

"It was terribly sad so many stars died, just for the sake of silliness. I'm no better than John Bonham or Keith Moon, just luckier. I'm not being a born-again Christian but you know... I quite enjoy not being high any more.**" 1989**

"I'm still having trouble with the drink problem. I stay home so I won't be tempted. I've managed to stave off the desire but it's a lot harder than people think. I just had to stop, so I go to Alcoholics Anonymous meetings twice a day, during the hours when the bars are open and I most need a drink." 1989

"I mean, I don't even like drinking... the feeling of being drunk is oblivion for me. I don't drink for the taste. I *hate* the taste! I drink it for oblivion from this planet, you know, get me off!**" 1989**

"For some reason the whole band got more and more into boozing when we got to Japan. And it's carried on right through Europe. The only reason I got back into it was because I couldn't shake this depression. In the end you say to yourself, what's the point of going through all this grief? Nothing's helping so I might as well have a drink. And of course the truth is that drink doesn't help you either. One drink leads to another and before you know it, it's the same old story again – Ozzy's drinking again! Ozzy's gone mad!" 1989

"I was like a mad dog chasing my tail.**"** **1989**

"It's a love affair I have with booze. It's like any addiction. You know it's killing you but you just can't put the stuff down. No alcoholic person out there goes, 'Oh shit yeah, I got pissed for a week. I don't want to talk about it.' And they amaze me... I mean Sharon used to drink a lot of booze many years ago. She got up one morning, we were in Monmouth, and she said 'Fucking hell, Ozzy, I feel like shit, I'm never gonna drink again.' And she's never drunk since, as far as I know." 1989

"I'll tell you what the worst addiction of my life is – tobacco. Old Holborn and Cuban cigars.**"** **1994**

"Morphine, demerol, valium, cocaine, barbiturates. I used to do a lot of grass and LSD back in the Black Sabbath days. One time I was out of my tree for a week talking to horses. And the weird thing was, they were talking back to me. But the worst was alcohol. I said to my mother once, 'Did dad drink much?' 'Yeah, but *nothing* like you!'" 1994

ULTIMATE SINS

"I always think of Lemmy when I see a can of Carlsberg Special... it's great stuff if you want a night out on the booze. The trick with this stuff isn't to start early on in the evening with it, but later on when you're ready to collapse. You don't last very long with this stuff, it's so strong... and that's speaking from experience.**"**

"I became a fit-drinker, I became a spasm-drinker. It's like when I was withdrawing one time I went into like a spasm because I didn't have a medical detox. This was about six months ago. It's not such a major thing. It doesn't mean I'm gonna have a heart attack. I'm pretty well healthy, I train every morning on my bike and I run around the field a bit. It's not as bad as it sounds, but if you've got a record of having these seizures they keep you on this medication. I'm on all kinds of medication."** 1989

"My time at the (Betty Ford) Clinic educated me. It was the first time I'd spent any time away from drink and drugs but, in this business you can't avoid a drink. And I've never been a born-again type of person. At least now I monitor it. If I say no, that's no for the whole day. If I have a drink, then it might as well be a bar full – I'll drink till I drop. But as long as you can accept being an alcoholic – and I am an alcoholic...**"** **1985**

"I've fucked up so many things through drugs and drink." 1989

"All I know is, I am an alcoholic and my name is Ozzy. And I've got to take certain steps to try and arrest the disease. Because I'm either gonna kill myself, kill someone else, which I very nearly did, or I'm

gonna go insane, I'm gonna be locked away in an insane asylum. It's got to the point now where I don't get happy-pissed, I go bulldozing around. I don't even know what I'm doing or where I'm at. Sharon says she's terrified when she sees me drink now. It upsets the whole family, close friends and everybody that works for me. **"** 1989

"I never set out to be a businessman, I just wanted to have fun, fuck chicks and do drugs!" 1997

" I should be dead by now. Most people imagine rock stars to have a great life. But success doesn't mean a fucking thing if you're an alcoholic. I've tried to stop drinking many times and receive therapy for it. Drinking is not glamorous, it's a killer. But over Christmas I went out a few times and got drunk. I can't stop myself – nor could Steve. He didn't drink for pleasure. He drank to escape. He had too much too soon and couldn't cope. He had it all – talent, nice houses and cars. Now he's dead at 30 and I think, 'There but for the grace of God go I.' **"**

1991, ABOUT THE DEATH OF HIS FRIEND, DEF LEPPARD'S STEVE CLARK

"There's not enough alcohol in the world for me. There's no such thing as moderation in Ozzy Osbourne's vocabulary. I've never had a pint in my life. It's all or nothing – whether it's drugs, sex, drink, falling in love, *anything*." 1997

" I've polluted every cell in my body with this crap, so my body gets pissed off when it can't get it. Someone said to me the other week, 'How long have you been drinking?' I told them 20 to 25 years. And they just looked at me and said, 'Are you surprised that you don't feel good in a week? It's taken you 25 years to get here, it ain't gonna take five minutes to get well again, is it?' **"** 1989

"I just couldn't stand it any more – the shakes, the horrors, the phone ringing thinking, 'Fuck, it's bad news', and that horrible feeling of blacking out. I'd get blackouts: my biggest nightmare was that someone would say, 'That's the man who ran over my husband last night', and I just wouldn't know." 1995

ULTIMATE SINS

"People say, 'Brilliant! Chicks! All the dope! All the booze! You have parties every night!' But it gets boring. I got to the point where I said, 'Why am I doing this?' I'm screwing some groupie and I think, 'What fucking disease have I caught now?' You know shitting myself, every two seconds looking at my dick seeing if it's still on me... it's absolutely not worth it for me. Half the time I wouldn't know whether I'd done it or not because I was so fucking out of it, and I'd get so guilty I'd get fucked up again. And I just got to the point where I thought, 'That booze has to go, that fucking lifestyle has to go.'" **1997**

"**I was frightened of living and frightened of dying, and that's a horrible place to be. I just didn't have the bottle to end it. I'd wake up in the morning and if I didn't have anything to worry about, I'd worry. And it would escalate into this incredible dark monster in my head, and the only escape I used to know was drugs and booze.**" 1995

"That was it. But then I started to feel this anxiety. It got so bad I started going to a shrink. They said to me, 'Ozzy you have a chemical imbalance in your brain, induced by chemical and alcohol abuse', and they put me on Prozac. I was like, 'What's the point of taking a pill if you don't get stoned?' But now, I don't turn into Charles Manson any more."

"**For many years I was trying to stop the booze and I couldn't stop it man, it was like a monkey on my back. I'm not one of those holier-than-thou fuckers, either. Believe me, if I thought I could successfully go to the fridge and get a can of beer and have a good old fucking laugh, then I would, but I know if I go to that beer then I'm fucking over. One's too many and ten's not enough.**" 1995

"I don't drink now 'cos I don't want to, but there's nothing worse than people preaching after they've given up drinking or taking drugs." **1997**

"I'm not saying I'm 100 per cent drug free, because I have to take this anti-depressant called Prozac. I've been taking it for the last three or four years now. What happens – and I've got this therapist I go to when I think it's necessary and tell him what's going on in my head – I still get that feeling, but it kind of nips it in the bud; it doesn't grow into this big ugly ogre. For many years it was like 'Wildman Ozzy Osbourne' or whatever, but underneath it all, there was this little wet fart going, 'Someone hold me together.'" 1995

"It was hell for me, that last tour: 14 months! Trying to get sober on the road is... Everybody I've met that's got sober said to me, 'Ozzy, you're heading for major destruction, you're heading for a major calamity.' But you haven't a chance on the road... I was whacking cortisone in me twice a month and all that shit just to keep going. And it's all mind-altering. It's all a drug. It's a steroid. I was fucking crazy when I came off that last tour! Absolutely insane! I'm still not sane now." 1989

"When I go on that stage it's like my fix; they get me through the day. I tend to beat myself up when I can't give them my heart and soul, when I've had a late night and I should have gone to bed, because I feel I've let them down. One of the things that curbed my drinking was the fact that it wasn't fair to my audience." 2001

"Why I'm alive I don't know. I remember when you'd run out of cocaine, you'd be scratching the carpet for anything that resembled the white stuff. It could be dog shit and you'd be putting it up your nose: 'Oh look, there's a rock!"' 2001

"One of the worst things about my drug abuse is that it's left me with a chemical imbalance for which I'll have to take stuff for the rest of my life – I'm on Prozac and anti-seizure medication. My old man used to say, 'You play now, you pay later.'" 1998

"I don't drink, I don't get stoned, and now my trainer says I've gotta stop drinking sodas. I might as well shoot myself in the face. There's fuck-all left, you know?" 2001

"I quit smoking this year, after 40 fucking years of trying. Being a singer, smoking's the worst possible thing you can do, you know? I still haven't smoked, so if I do a bad show now it's not my fault." 2001

ULTIMATE SINS

"In the old days when I used to drink I'd wake up in the morning thinking, 'I don't know my name, I don't know where you're from and I know I'm not the first guy you've done this week.' Then, when Aids started I just thought, 'Forget it.' I was seeing guys coming out of the clap clinic thanking God that they'd only caught syphilis." 1998

"One time I bought a pound of grass and took four tablets of mescalin, a quarter of an ounce of cocaine and a bottle of tequila and I was out of my tree for a week. I had the worst fucking time of my entire life. I thought, 'That's it, I've done it now, I'm going to be here forever.'" 2000

"I remember the first time I had coke – it was on tour with Mountain in the States. Being from England we wouldn't touch coke, heroin, or acid even, it was just dope. But by then Mountain had the Learjet, the jewellery, the chicks and they were stars. We were herberts from Birmingham by comparison." 2001

"I used to smoke all the time when I was younger. It seems to have become so strong nowadays, I hate the feeling. We used to smoke stuff that would make us giggle and give us the munchies. Now it's like being on acid: 'When's it gonna end? When's it gonna end?'" 2001

"My biggest addiction these days is exercise. I run every day. I'll probably be next to Jimmy Savile next year running the fucking marathon! I only take pills now for clinical reasons, not to get stoned any more. All the stuff I did left me with some neurological problems – I'm a manic depressive, a nutter. Sharon says she'll second that." 2000

"Did you ever meet Betty Ford? Yeah. I met her a couple of times. She was a very quiet lady. She'd come in like royalty, have the unit polished. She was all right, though. She'd hover like a blow-up doll at one end of the wing and then go out the other. It was, like, 13 Hail Bettys, and she'd go home." 2001

ULTIMATE SINS

“We had this guy follow us with a suitcase of cocaine! I'm not kiddin'. This fella literally had a whole suitcase of the stuff and we all knew that wherever we were he'd only be a few hundred yards away in his car.” **2001**

“I know I should be dead. I didn't burn the candle at both ends – I burnt it every fucking which way the fucking thing can be held!”

2001

“Nowadays it's all mineral water, back then it was two cases of Dom Perignon, a case of Hennessey... beer, drugs, everything. I was doing four bottles of brandy a day and as much cocaine, pot and champagne as I could handle. I was out of control. We used to order a banquet every night, and we'd end up wasting most of it in food fights.” **1998**

“I mixed some medication I'd been prescribed by a psychiatrist with alcohol and I just black out. I woke up the next day (3 September 1989) in Amersham police station and I honestly didn't know what was going on. The copper said, 'Do you know why you're here?' and they told me I'd threatened to kill my wife. After that I vowed to lock myself up in rehab until I was right again. But when I came out I drank again, I couldn't stop, I was a mess...” 1998

“I don't plan a day. I'm not one of those organised people. I'm a TV addict: I love the History Channel and Discovery Channel, TLC, A&E. This year, I've had one of the greatest achievements of my entire life: I haven't picked up a cigarette in five months. I mean, I was into coke and booze, but cigarettes were the hardest to quit, by far.”

2001

Ozzy At 'Ome

THE FAMILY MAN WITH WIFE & KIDS

"What turns me on? A good cup of coffee in the morning.**"** 2001

"Have you seen the movie *Meet The Parents*? It's so fucking funny, it's not true. That goofy Ben Stiller character – my wife said he reminds her of me." 2001

"I always cry when me and my wife go and see slurpy movies. I'm there in the cinema with red eyes and tears rolling down my cheeks, and the kids are coming up and saying, 'Hey Ozzy, Satan rules!'**"** 2001

"When I was in England recently I was working out on my exercise bike, watching breakfast television. And they did a piece about an American girl called Eva Cassidy, who died of cancer. She's got an album with a cover of 'Over The Rainbow' on it. I was sat there, tears rolling down , and ended up buying four copies of the CD."

2001

"I'm actually a very quiet person at home. I like to potter around the garden.**"** 1991

"What makes me happy is playing with my dogs and animals, and riding my motorbikes. I work out a lot... when I'm in England I like (satellite TV channel) UK Gold, because I've never seen those old shows – I was always on the road. I catch up with *The Bill*.

OZZY *Talking*

OZZY *Talking*

I was watching a re-run of *Shaft* the other night in Prague, and the language and the hair-dos were wild! Everyone had maracas and bongos – and I've never seen anyone in New York with maracas and bongos. But then, they're still listening to Led Zeppelin in Prague.**"** 1997

"I don't wake up in the morning, I'm shot into the world, and my happiest place is in my sleep. That's why I used to get stoned and drunk all the time. I'm more pessimistic than optimistic, and if it wasn't for my wife, I wouldn't be here now. She's the loving boot up the arse I need now and again. A love tap. If I had my way, I'd just stay in my room and rot the rest of my life.**"** **1997**

"I'm John Osbourne now... You've got no fear of me being fucking Ozzy Osbourne around here – because if I am, Sharon goes, 'Fuck off. Go and soak your head in the horse trough and don't come back until you've found your brains.'**"** 1988

"I've become a bit of a Howard Hughes these days.**"** **1995**

"When I got divorced from my first wife I said, 'I've come for my clothes' and I got two bin-bags with all these platform boots in and I threw them in the trash bin. I should have kept them – they'll sell for a fortune at Sotheby's. Some of them I've given away to be auctioned for charity – then this guy, Tony, who's now working for me, bought one of them at an auction, so the fucking thing's ended up back in my house! Remember when I used to wear that stupid chain-mail suit? Or that dumb glitter outfit in the Eighties? I looked like Liberace.**"** 2000

His wife/manager Sharon Arden

"She saved my life.**"** 1998

"I was sitting in this apartment in California and thinking, 'Oh dear it's all over, I'm finished. I'll be back in Birmingham working in the abattoir again. I thought my life had ended and I was just getting drunk and stoned all day every day for three months and I was like living knee-deep in cartons of empty cigarette packets and all the rest of the shit with the curtains closed. A fucking fat stupid mess I was. Fat and stupid and drugged.

"Then, to my amazement, Sharon just appeared one day and said, 'You've got to get yourself together because we've got rid of Sabbath and we want to take you on.' Whaat? I was amazed. Sharon and me had nothing going at the time – in actual fact, she was seeing Tony Iommi – but there she was.**"** 1988

"If it wasn't for Sharon I'd be dead now without doubt. Career-wise, I would definitely be dead – and I would almost certainly have been physically dead as well. She was the first person in my life who had ever come along and given me any encouragement because in Sabbath I was the least meaningful member of the band.

"But Sharon came along, showed me respect and gave me encouragement – she educated me in my cleanliness and my mannerisms and my attitude and everything. She made me grow up and I just fell in love with her because she's great. And she sorted out all the business because, with business, I like to do as little as possible.**"**

1988

DAUGHTER KELLY AND
WIFE SHARON

OZZY AT 'OME

"I just wanted to set the record straight... I picked up the newspaper and I read 'Ozzy gets divorced', and it's not that at all! I mean Sharon was round this afternoon. I asked her then, 'Are you going to divorce me?' She said, 'Absolutely not.' And I want to say that I'm not gonna let people from the outside fuck my marriage up. Nobody thought we'd last as long as we have. I hope to God that we last as long as the rest of our lives."

1989

"You know what I've learnt from my old lady? That people are never dead in this business. Someone of 95 could come out with a hit LP and it doesn't have to be as good as their old stuff or anything."

"The most important thing in the whole world to me right now is my wife and kids." 1989

"Do you know me and Sharon once went to look at Roger Whittaker's house in England – when we were looking for somewhere to buy – and it's fuckin' *huge*. He's got this huge place out in Essex with this bloody great sports complex built on to the side. It's amazing! We never bought it though... but we did have a shit in his toilet... me and Sharon! We both shat in Roger Whittaker's toilet! It's a pity his toothbrush wasn't in there as well, you could have had a go on that too... yeah, but I did wipe my arse on his curtains!"

"Sharon gives me tough love and she's also given me some tremendous bollockings when I needed it. She's not just some Pamela Anderson figure, she's very conservative, hard-working woman. I have no desire for anyone else." 1998

"Sharon's never cooked a fucking dinner in her life – thank God for Domino's pizzas, I say. And with three teenage kids it's hard to have sex – they say, 'We know what you're doing in there you dirty pair of old bastards' or 'We can't go in there, Dad's dry-humping mum again.' If I'd dared to say what they say to my dad I'd be lying in the garden with a pitchfork stuck in my fucking chest." **2000**

His Kids

"I've got three beautiful kids at home. I don't fucking hang upside down from the rafters when I get home and drink fucking nun's piss and all this bollocks. It's just a job. It's like a clown at a circus. I mean the amount of guns that's sold every day. How can they send kids to Vietnam and then say my fucking music is Satanic?"

1989

"I took my son (Jack) on stage in Long Beach. Now every time he comes down, he wants to go on stage. People ask me if I'd want him to follow in my footsteps. Musically I wouldn't mind, but I wouldn't recommend the abuse I've put my body through. I've been in a lot of treatment centres, but that's just part of the job. The stress part of the job is immense – and I can't handle stress."

THE OSBOURNES: JACK, AIMEE, KELLY, SHARON AND OZZY

" ... he's desperate to get up there with me. Sharon usually has to hold him back at the side of the stage whenever he comes to one of the shows. He walked on stage at the Long Beach Arena on New Year's Eve, clutching his teddy and singing along to everything. I was so proud! He's a real chip off the old block. Absolutely fuckin' loves running around on that stage. "

"Girls. I've got no idea. The eldest one, Kelly's 12, she's coming to that funny age, you know mood swings. " 1994, ABOUT HIS DAUGHTER

"Well, there's only so much you can do as a parent. As long as they're happy, and the person's not being abusive and they don't think they're on to an easy meal 'cos they're dating the daughter of a rock star or whatever. "

1997, ON THE MAN WHO FIRST DATES HIS ELDEST DAUGHTER

"I'm a parent, and there's nothing else that's more sacred to me than my wife and children, you know. You go, nothing will ever happen to my kids; they won't get HIV, they won't get cancer. But it does happen, and going to the Make-A-Wish Foundation really made me thank God for the life that I have here. " 2001

"I'd feel honoured if one of my kids wanted to follow in my footsteps but imagine if she sounded like me? You have to look at the downside as well. I love Julian Lennon but everyone keeps on about how he sounds too much like his dad. But if their hearts were in it, I'd support my kids in anything they wanted to do. " 1998

"Sharon's the boss, without any shadow of a doubt. The kids discipline me. Try to discipline them, but they go, 'Oh fuck you.' But one of the things rock'n'roll had done for me is that my kids know I do not fuck around when it comes to giving advice. I just say, 'Look, you do this. You do that. and this is what's gonna fuck it up if you do that.' You cannot afford to be anything but brutally honest. " 2001

OZZY AT 'OME 🙶

Ozzy In The Kitchen

"I make the greatest chips on the planet. My kids come running in yelling, 'Dad's making chips!' when I get the chip pan out." 1997

"I'd love to be able to cook like Keith Floyd."

"I'm now a vegetarian. Just in the last month or so, because I read so much fucking shit lately about meat. But I'm not worried about all that animal shit: I'm not like Linda McCartney and I'm not going to start making fucking Ozzy vegetable pies. Next to Paul and Linda's stuff, fake bat burgers! I change my diet from time to time, and I just decided to stop eating meat because I went for a medical and my cholesterol level was quite high. But if I'm hungry and I'm in the middle of a freeway, and the only thing to eat is a meat pie, I'll whap that down my trap, no trouble. If I'm that hungry, I'll eat a *person*!" 1997

"What can I actually cook? Well, last time I tried to cook some chips the pan caught light, and the flames nearly set the house on fire." 2001

Home & Abroad

OZZY'S WORLD TRAVELS

❝I like America but I wouldn't live there because (a) there's a lot of guns about and a lot of people who would use them and (b) I don't want to be in the firing line. I'm frightened of the violence. The films! You want to see the films over there, man! They've got this bizarre thing called *Rollerball*. Have you heard about that? It's fucking nuts, man! It's bananas! And the audience always start clapping and cheering when the gruesome bits come. They'll have gladiators over there soon, you wait. It's like the rise and fall of the Roman Empire. It's *incredible*.❞ **1975**

❝**I love the American way of life. Let's be honest, what's Britain got now? English people are just paying for politicians' fuck-ups. They should have a Maggie Thatcher Burning Night instead of Guy Fawkes. Her head's full of shit. And to think I once voted for her to give a woman a chance... politicians are scumbags. They're all fucked. What about the people? The fucking mass unemployment? I tell ya, I predict a bloody revolution over there. People say I've got power over people, I should make a stand – but that's not up to me...**

❝**Don't get me wrong, I'm not Communist, far from it, there's just got to be a better way of living. We can't even educate people about the dangers of nuclear war. Over here there's fall-out shelters everywhere. Who's got 'em in Britain? The politicians and the very few. What about us?❞** 1981

OZZY *Talking*

"I love the climate in America, you can get anything you want. Snow for skiing, sun for sunbathing, you can go anywhere you like. And there's some lovely countryside here. I love it here, although I don't think I could ever live full-time in the US. The thing is about going back to England is that it's quieter and calmer and I can collect myself more easily. As it happens, Malibu is one of my favourite places ever – better than Hawaii, better than anywhere in the States." **1989**

"I lived in the South of France once on tax exile and I couldn't stand it 'cos you couldn't see the fucking beach. The people looked like fucking orang-utans, all these topless beaches and fat birds with their tits hanging out. Personally, I've never really had that great a time in France." 1989

"It's a very sad thing for me that we have to leave England. Because of the state of the economics of this country we're being forced to go. We cannot afford to function under these tax things so we'll have to join the rest and wave bye-bye... it must sound as if everybody in the rock business is tight and they don't want to share the money, but it's not like that. People in the business have a limited amount of time. You're only young once and I can't be doing Black Sabbath when I'm 58. I don't expect to be the wild kid from Aston when I'm that age.

"I don't want to be wealthy for the rest of my life, I want to be comfortable. I want to sit and dedicate myself to music in whatever way it comes out, but with all these tax laws, at the age of 38 we'll probably have to sign back on the dole again. I don't think we deserve that." **1975**

"If Bill Clinton can't get a blow job off his secretary then he's in the wrong job."

"I thought it was a plastic toy so I just grabbed this thing, bit the head off and thought 'Fuck me! It was flapping...'"

"

"I believe I'm going nuts. But so what? As long as I'm enjoying it!"

"I never set out to be a businessman, I just wanted to have fun, fuck chicks and do drugs!"

"My only ambition in the world is to go to Egypt, stand on top of the Central Pyramid and piss all over it." 1981

"I've bought a house in Buckinghamshire and, in the two-and-a-half years since I bought it, I must have been there about three months at the most! I mean, what's the point in me buying all this property and buying all this stuff if I'm never there to appreciate it?**"** 1989

"We often think about moving to America because it would be easier because we spend so much time here. At the start of tours I often have the thought, we'll move. But by the end I just wanna get back to the house in England, get outta here and into the quiet."

"Being married and with the kids, the thing that terrifies me the most is the drug and crime situation in America. I watched this television thing with this ex-cop all about these serial killers... fucking frightening it was. One guy they haven't caught has killed 14 people!**"** 1989

"It's breaking my heart to sell this place (his home in Little Chalfont, Bucks) because we've done great things with it. But we have had problems with the neighbours. There's a prat at the end of the drive who's convinced I put a security camera on the wall so I can see in his bedroom.
"I don't know anybody else here except our gardener. We just mind our own business. The great thing about LA is that everyone minds their own business too. Apart from Sharon not getting on with the neighbours, I was worried that I had become a telephone father to my kids because I've spent 18 months out of the last two years in LA. I feel like Uncle Ozzy who comes back bearing presents. It was getting me really depressed. But we shan't live in LA forever because when the kids get older I don't want them buying drugs in the local supermarket. It's like Cocaine City."

1991

HOME & **ABROAD**

❝If anyone gets into my house out there I would have no hesitation in blowing his head off. I've never kept a gun in the house in England, but I will keep one in LA.❞ **1991**

❝**I've got no desire to go the Middle East, forget it! I don't give a fuck if my career's down the toilet, you won't get me doin' Uriah Heep-style 'around the world in 80 days' tours of Beirut, Bygong, Gongbong and all that fucking rubbish.❞** 1989

❝You wanna know one of the most disappointing places I've ever been to in my life? Rio De Janeiro in Brazil! This was for that Rock in Rio Festival. I get there and expect to see all these beautiful girls and stuff... and it was fucking disgusting. I was very unhappy. I'd never seen poverty like it. From the airport our driver was saying to us, 'I wish you would not take pictures of the hill, it is not a very good representation of our country or city', and this whole hill was covered in shanty houses, sheds that people lived in. Fucking hell!❞ **1989**

❝**When I went to Japan I was fucking amazed... you hold on to a bar and dump through a hole in the floor in some of these Oriental toilets. On the Japanese Bullet Trains they have oriental toilets and Western ones. Check out the oriental ones and you'll fucking crack up! A bar, two moulded footprints and a hole to shit in. The golden shot!❞** 1989

❝I've just got back to LA and I'm so glad to have escaped foot and mouth, the Cowschwitz, in England. It's so fuckin' sad for the farmers I'm thinking of doing some kind of Farm Aid benefit – like Live Aid. Although there wouldn't be any land we could hold it on, so we'd have to do it in a 747 flying round and round England.❞

2001

Sabs Speak Out!

THE OTHERS AIR THEIR VIEWS ON OZZY

Tony Iommi

"I used to hate the sight of him. I couldn't stand him, and I used to beat him up whenever I saw him. We just didn't get on at school. He was a little punk." **1998**

"Bill and I were looking for a singer, and we spotted this advert that said 'Singer looking for a gig. Call Ozzy...' I said to Bill, 'I know an Ozzy... it can't possibly be that one.' So we went to the address listed in the ad, and knocked on the door. Sure enough Ozzy appeared. I said to Bill, 'Forget it, forget it.' But Bill wanted to chat with him. We talked, but when we left I said, 'No way, Bill, I know him.' Three weeks later, we ended up together anyway. Life moves in mysterious ways." 1998

TONY IOMMI

"He had a good career. He did really well to go out on his own and do what he did." 1998

"We knew we had to bring in somebody else. Geezer and Bill would say to me, 'Either Ozzy goes, or we go.' At that point, Bill was becoming the businessman of the band, with his briefcase and his haircut, and he fucking goes and tells Ozzy, 'Tony wants to get rid of you.' Ozzy always thought that I fired him on my own, when it was really the other two who wanted him out. But I wasn't too pleased with Ozzy either." 1998

Bill Ward

"Ronnie Dio is a musician, he can arrange a lot better than Ozzy could... he's got a lot of qualities which Ozzy had as well. He blends perfectly into the band. I saw Oz the other week and he's fine, he's doing his own thing... about this time last year he wasn't looking after himself, his health. Stuff like that. We really couldn't get along, that was the reason it went out of the window with Oz. We checked a few people and Ronnie just seemed to fit." 1980

"I wouldn't want to share a room with Ozzy now, though, because he's fucking nuts!" 1998

Geezer Butler

"He keeps on going on about how we shouldn't have kept the name after he left. He reckons he wrote all the songs, he thinks he thought of the name originally. And lately he's been saying we had to pay him off to leave the band. All that is totally ridiculous. It's a shame he has taken this kind of attitude because he's successful in his own right now." 1982

"I didn't like his first (solo record) at all. I think the new one (*Diary Of A Madman*) is quite good but the new guitarist is too much like Eddie Van Halen – you know, a pain in the arse." 1982

"There was nothing new coming out of the numbers Ozzy was doing in the last days of the band with him. But when Ronnie (Dio) came in he really made a hell of a difference." 1981

"I like a lot of Ozzy's solo stuff. I always knew he had it in him but it didn't always come out in Sabbath." 1997

"Will we do some solos so that Ozzy can have a breather? No fucking chance. He'll be all right. Most Sabbath songs have about one minute singing and five minutes of riffing." 1998

Ronnie Dio

"I never had the intention of trying to fill his shoes – that wasn't the point at all. I never considered trying to imitate him because he has a special kind of character which is just completely outgoing onstage. He was always someone to relate to because he was a punter – just like everyone in the audience. I can't do that, that's not my background and experience... I'm not saying that I'm better than Ozzy, nor am I suggesting I'm worse.

"When I sing those classic Black Sabbath songs it's not a question of Ronnie Dio giving everyone a break by doing his superstar versions of them. I'm just a person trying to put his own style of feeling into those songs." 1980

Cozy Powell

"We've deliberately kept a low profile, because there's been so much crap and trash that has been written about Black Sabbath, it's almost farcical. There's been so much written; it's been amazing! Ozzy – who's our press agent, by the way – I didn't really want to let it out of the bag, but I'm gonna have to tell somebody! We've had Ozzy on a retainer for the last two years. He's been absolutely brilliant – better press than we could ever have given ourself!" 1989

REUNION LINE UP...
(L-R) WARD, IOMMI, BUTLER AND OSBOURNE

SABS SPEAK OUT!

No Rest For The Wicked

HIS COMPULSION TO KEEP ON ROCKIN'

"I'm a rock'n'roll gypsy. I'll never give up. The only time I ever stopped was after Sabbath split. It took me a long time to get over it, after all it was 11 years of my life, and I really got ripped off. I lost six million pounds revenue through fuck-ups and rip-offs. After the split I just sat and got pissed and stoned for six weeks. But this band's given me reason to go on." 1981

"The will's still there to do it, but sometimes the body just goes, 'Sorry old son, you just ain't got it tonight.' Sometimes I go up there and I feel like I've got two left feet. I feel clumsy, y'know? But it's like Zakk says to me, if I thought every gig was brilliant, I'd never know the real thing when it happened." 1989

"Since 1968 I'd been at it – recording, touring, nearly non-stop. I was beginning to feel like a mouse on wheels. Trapped. So I took three years off, bought a new house, spent some time with my kids. I tried retirement but it sucked. It's a romantic idea but it doesn't work in reality. So I'm back doing the only thing I know how." 1995

"I'm comin' up to 21 successful years in rock'n'roll, but it just doesn't seem that long. Those ten years with Sabbath, I went to school, went through my teens and was in the band, then I couldn't see beyond or after Black Sabbath. And now I've been away for ten years, I can't imagine what the fuck was goin' on

in my head to make me think that. I suppose it's because I'm one of these guys who never thinks it's gonna get any better, a pessimist." 1989

"When I'm off the road I wanna be on the road, and when I'm on the road I can't wait to get off it. What I'd like is to have one really big album, like a Def Leppard LP or something, and then I could knock the whole idea of these big, long tours on the head." **1989**

"I get resentful when I'm away for too long a time. My kid starts to walk, my kid goes to school, my kid takes place in the school sports and I'm never there for any of it! I mean, I get on the phone – 'Aimée came second in a race at school today.' And I go, 'Oh wow, great. What the fuck you telling me for?' You could tell me Aimée just became the first child cosmonaut! I wouldn't know anything about it." 1989

"Well, I never really went into 'retirement' as such. I mean I'm always making these stupid, dumb fucking statements, and then I wonder, 'What the fuck did I say that for?' I got to this point on the last tour where I didn't wanna be a mouse on a wheel, I wanted to know what it was like to be off, to not be living on a schedule. I did the No More Tears tour, then I wondered, 'What the fuck do I do now?' What is retirement? I mean, Bob Hope ain't fucking retired and he's ninety fucking four or something.

"It's not like a job you can retire from. I mean if you do a job that you hate and you're miserable in it, and you hate the pay cheque and you go home to a miserable existence, then I understand people saying, 'Ten more years and I'm fucking outta here.' But in all reality, how can you retire from a job that isn't a job? I don't think there's a better way to make a living." **1995**

NO REST FOR THE WICKED

"I can't stand having a lot of people backstage. I hate a full dressing room. It drives me mad... I hate loads of people around backstage. We had that when Sabbath played in Birmingham."

1998

"To my fans: As you will have seen in this week's *Sounds*, I have reluctantly had to cancel my British tour due to nervous exhaustion. This has happened as a result of a very long and arduous six-month non-stop tour of America, illness and a number of personal problems all of which has meant the doctors saying, 'Stop – enough is enough.' I cannot tell you how very, very sorry I am at having to do this especially as I have been looking forward to playing to my British fans, there's no place like home.

"As you know, I regard my fans as the most important people in my life, you and you alone are the ones who have stuck by me through thick and thin and without you there probably would be no Ozzy Osbourne. Had there been any way of carrying on I would have done so, as I really feel that I have let you down badly. But I shall be back, I promise, with a show like you've never seen before and I hope you'll still all be there as you've always been in the past. I love you all and I'm sorry." DECEMBER 1981, FULL PAGE AD IN SOUNDS

"Happiness doesn't come from high finance, though. It helps a great deal. I mean, people say, 'I'd rather be wealthy and unhappy than poor and unhappy.' And I'm not going to give it to some far-off fucking charities, you can forget that!" 1989

"It made me a nervous wreck to think that there were people out there who were determined enough to kill me. When we played Dallas one time I had to play wearing a bulletproof vest because there was one nutter who was hounding me. I recently found out that they'd caught him and he was a clinical psychotic." 2001

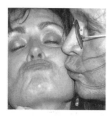

"I'm not at my best until my eyeballs are fucking bulging out of my head with panic. I don't know why, but I come up with good stuff when I'm under pressure." 2001

OZZY *Talking*

“I'm an okay showman and an okay entertainer, I've never pretended to be anything more than that.” 1998

“In 32 years I've never been out of work. What happens is whenever the music gets boring they'd bring out 'Smoke On The Water' and 'Paranoid'. Over here in the States they're all getting rhinestone fucking Ozzy T-shirts and studding up old clothes. I'm just glad I've got a market to play to.” 2000

“The tour starts on Halloween and we've got a black-clothed Santa Claus strapped up on a crucifix behind the stage! We're also going to have a black advent calendar with pictures of Santa being butt-fucked!” 2001

“The first thing I'd like to say to these bodyguards I'm supposed to need is 'no weapons, no coshes, no handcuffs and no aggression' because their job is to keep aggression away. These twats don't think they're doing their fucking jobs right if they haven't broken someone's arm for two weeks. But if they do hurt someone it isn't them the kids thinks has hurt them, it becomes 'Ozzy Osbourne broke my arm.' It all reflects on me. I couldn't hurt a fly so I can't have people like that around me.” 2001

Fans&Groupies

HOW OZZY RELATES TO HIS FOLLOWERS

"There was this shady guy with dark eyes at one of the gigs. He said, 'Can I have a word with you privately?' I thought, 'I've got a real zocko here.' He had eyes like sheep's twats. He said, 'I've been following you for years' and I said, 'I'm glad you finally found me.' He said, 'I've got a problem, man. I've been into black magic for years, what should I do?' I said, 'Change to Milk Tray, it's a new cult.' I think instead of wearing my cross, I'll have a big box of chocolates on stage." 1980

"Sometimes it freaks you out. Most of them are out of their brains on God knows what. D'you see that sod who asked me to kiss him? I wouldn't have minded if he didn't have a beard... Before Las Vegas it was like 110 degrees and this guy came up to me like a monk on acid, he was wearing monk's gear and these bloody big boots, he was staring at me trying to freak me out, so I just pulled a worse face at him and freaked him out.

"A bloke walked up once and said, 'I give great head, man.' I told him to piss off and the bastard spent the night outside my hotel room. You get nutters all the time, one guy kept trying to give us his girlfriend. Bill Ward couldn't handle it when we were in Sabbath. He used to go round wearing plastic glasses and moustache so no-one would recognise him, with a cap gun in his pocket..." 1981

OZZY Talking

❝I've got this one nutcase who plagues me in America. He calls himself The Lord God. He phones my office thousands of times and I don't know why. This guy is a 22-carat fucking nutcase. He's fucking mad. He sent me Polaroid pictures of his baby in a big pair of boots and writes Fairies Wear Boots on it. He's painted my name all over his fucking house, his car and his drive. He's built a fucking tomb that he expects me to go and spend the rest of eternity in. He is fucking *out there*!❞ 1995

❝**This geezer came up to me with a sword on stage once, but me road manager bashed him with a mike stand.**❞ 1981

❝There was this bird once who I thought I'd pulled. I thought she was a bit funny 'cos she didn't smoke or drink. When she got back to the hotel room she started on about being a redeemer and how I was polluted and how she was gonna save my soul... she learnt how to fly in less than a minute.❞ 1981

❝**Groupies are great fun at first, but then it gets a little bit tiring. You fuck maybe nine or ten of them, then one day you say, 'Leave me alone, I'm human, I've got feelings.' I've had them. I've fucked them off – I'm not saying I'm a goody-goody. I'll fuck around, I'll do whatever I want to do. We used to have all-night parties and line them up. But you got to sleep, you got to eat.**
❝**Doing that for ten years, baby, it does you in. I'm telling you. For them to see me up there on stage for an hour-and-a-half, sometimes I have to go through a lot of shit. Like you're dying in the day and you've got to take this and shove this up your arse and that up your nose, have your B12 shots and *this* vitamin and that vitamin. You end up like a fucking rattle.**❞ 1978

❝They took me to a hospital in New Orleans once and I came round to find this guy on his hands and knees by the side of my bed going, 'Psst, are you Ozzy Osbourne? Are you dying?' I said, 'I don't know.' He said, 'Before you do, can you give me your autograph?' And shoves this piece of paper into my hand. No respect, these fuckers.❞ 1998

Sons Of The Sabbath

OZZY'S VIEWS ON THOSE HE'S INSPIRED

Lita Ford

"I think 'Close My Eyes Forever' (their duet) is a great track and I'm thrilled that it's doing so well. But if it goes Top 10, that'll be enough to make me happy. Me and Lita have both had singles that have done reasonably well over there, but neither of us has ever had a Top 10 American single... I had a lot of fun making that record with Lita. If she wants to do another one, I've got something in the pipeline, as long as we don't turn into the Peters and Lee of Heavy Metal." 1989

Def Leppard

"A great band, man, Christ knows what they'll do to us tonight." 1981

DEF LEPPARD

(Christian Rockers) Stryper

"I think they are the biggest bunch of phoney muthafuckers. If they sent their royalties to some religious sect, fair enough. I don't pretend to be anything I'm not. I'm not the anti-Christ and I don't try and turn people into frogs by playing rock music. They are just playing rock'n'roll and using God to sell their music."

New Metal

"I don't listen to many new bands. I prefer to listen to bands that made me want to play. Early Zeppelin, Free, bands like that. It's so busy now, it's really hard to keep in touch. I do like The Prodigy and I like Fear Factory, as it happens. But I don't know how Burton (C Bell) does what he does – growling and screaming and smoking all the time." 1997

Metallica

"When I was touring with Metallica, I thought they were taking the piss when they were playing all the old Sabbath hits in their dressing room. I pulled them up on it and said, 'What the fuck do you think you're doing? I'm being nice to you guys.' I got it all wrong, because they loved Sabbath, but what I was made to feel from the Black Sabbath years was that we were worthless."
1997

METALLICA

Faith No More

❝I like this band. I did 'War Pigs' with them once at some party in LA, and it was a riot. I forgot the words and their singer had to come in and help me! Not that he knows the fucking words either...❞

Marilyn Manson

❝You take all the fucking bras and suspenders and all the dildos... you take all those things away and *can they play*? I mean all this Bible burning, we used to do that in fucking '71! Just to have something to do! We'd get drunk and fucking burn the Gideon's Bible in the hotel room!❞ 1997

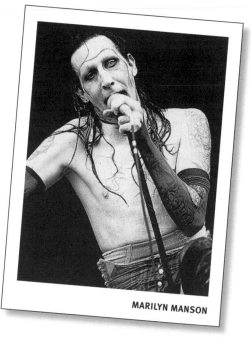

MARILYN MANSON

On The Sabbath Tribute Album 'Nativity In Black'

❝First of all, I felt like a dick when someone asked me to sing on an album that was a tribute to my own work. I felt kind of like, 'How dare I do this to me!' Like, 'Hey, wait a minute, isn't this a bit big-headed, man?' But at the end of the day, to make time enough to remember there was a Black Sabbath, I suppose that's something to be proud of... but (starts singing) 'Nobody does it better...'❞ 1994

That Ol' Black Magic

THOUGHTS ON THE BAND'S VARIOUS RE-FORMATIONS

The Live Aid Reunion

❝I said, 'Absolutely no, no way, not at all. I mean why? Why have I spent so much time breaking away from all that, only to... I've got a big, no bigger following now than I ever had with Black Sabbath. Why turn the clock back? Why give those guys a break?' It was like a Catch-22 situation. I couldn't get away from it then. I mean if I back out, I'll be the only artist in the world to turn around and say 'fuck it!' and that's a situation I don't want.

❝My life's been reasonably peaceful for the last 18 months; I don't want people to saying, 'Look at this fucking moron, he wouldn't play for Ethiopia!' People don't want to work with you. So I'll do it. I won't take it seriously though! I'm going to phone Ian Gillan up and ask him for his piece of paper that he used to read the lyrics off onstage.❞ **1985**

❝**There was a romantic notion at one point that maybe we could see if Sabbath worked again. But I got on that stage, and I gotta confess, this whole black cloud had followed us again. It was over – the cement was on the fucking box – that was when I knew there'd never be a chance of us getting back together.**❞ 1990

❝And I am definitely, *definitely* not rejoining Black Sabbath. And that's from the bottom of my heart. You can kiss that one straight off. I will never rejoin Black Sabbath. No fucking way! Not in this life or the next...❞ **1989**

OZZY *Talking*

On The Live Reunion In 1997

❝I'm bringing the OzzFest to Britain. Finsbury Park, London. August 30. It's gonna be me and Black Sabbath, Marilyn Manson, Pantera, Type O Negative, Machine Head and Neurosis. It'll be fucking great! All we can hope for is that it's sunny. I don't care if a fucking atom bomb goes off, it's still gonna be awesome.❞ **1997**

❝**I'm 49 this year and every year I hear the same thing: when are Sabbath going to get together again? The funny thing is, when we were together everyone hated us! I used to say to Sharon, 'Do you really think it'll happen?' And for ages there were too many chiefs and not enough Indians, but now all that bullshit's in the past.❞** 1997

❝I don't even know if the chemistry is still there. I can't plan ahead. But I can put all my irons in the fire and see what happens.❞ **1997**

❝**We gave each other space and respect, and it worked. All the juvenile shit-slinging, slagging and petty jealousies have finally gone. We're too fucking old, and I think we all realise the strengths we have together when we're on that stage...❞** 1997

❝We don't even need to rehearse 'cos we know the songs so well. For a live album, we'll only need to tape one show, two at the most.❞ **1997**

❝**I've said it many times before, but it's a weird deal. There's something magical between Tony Iommi, Geezer Butler and myself that is beyond explaining. It's this invisible fucking magic that just happens when we're up there... For the future, I don't know, none of us have really discussed it yet. I am open to take it to the next stage, but I don't know what either Tony or Geezer think yet.'** 1997

On The Late Nineties
'Reunion'/'Last Supper' Shows

"A lot has changed. We don't have time to start pissing around like nancy boys. There's something magical about us playing together. We've been rehearsing a bit recently – and I'm not bullshitting, but there's no point in us rehearsing. We know it all backwards. Those songs are our roots." 1997

"The second night at the NEC was one of the most amazing things I've ever done in my life. There may be 20 shows I'll take with me to the grave, and that was one of them." 1998

"In the old days we'd do a few songs, then have a guitar break, do a few more songs, then have a drum break. When we did the OzzFest last year, that was 50 minutes. This was a two-hour stretch. But it was a lot of fun. And the crowd were fucking amazing." 1998

"It's so nice to come full circle and be friends again."

"We've all grown up. It's so good to have a laugh and a joke about some of the crazy things we used to get up to. Everybody's matured. If any of us don't want to do something, we just say our piece and leave." 1998

"The magic is still there... I find a lot of the press people are fishing for things like 'You said this about Iommi', or 'Iommi said this about you.' Whether I did or whether I didn't doesn't matter. It was a long time ago. Get over it. For fuck's sake, if that was the case, nobody would speak to anyone who was fucking German because of the war." 1998

"Over the years I've had various line-ups covering Sabbath classics like 'Iron Man', 'Paranoid', 'War Pigs' and the rest. And they've all been good players, but it's nothing like the real thing. I've always said that there's no-one better than Tony for coming out with riffs. You can't beat the originals." 1998

"When I played with Sabbath in December, I realised the difference between my solo stuff and Sabbath songs. They're light years apart. It made me realise how special this band is." 1998

"If there was no public demand, we wouldn't do it. But there is a public demand. I still get a buzz out of playing the songs and it still sounds as good now as it did then, whether I'm singing about Satan coming round the bend or *me* going round the fucking bend."
1998

"I can't say whether it's the final, final show ever unless one of us dies. I shouldn't say that. Last time I said, 'Well at least we're all still alive,' and Bill Ward dropped to the floor with a heart attack! He's doing fine now – though we do have to kick-start him before we do a show.' 2000

On The OzzFest

" The idea of the OzzFest was just to bring some real hard rock back to the UK. People keep saying that rock music is over, that it's dead. They're saying it all the time in America but I don't see it. Every show I played in America last year was a sell-out so how can rock be dead? "

1997

" It's only in the last ten years that we've realised what kind of impact (Sabbath) had. We did the OzzFest in the summer, and while we were on all the other bands would be on the stage headbanging. I couldn't believe it. It made me think, 'Fucking hell, what did we have?' " 1997

" The OzzFest is just about giving kids value for money. We got the best bands we could get to make it a really great day. "

" You know, last year they were all saying we were out of our minds, that nobody would care about a heavy-music festival. Well, we ended up selling 50,000 tickets over two gigs. Then these promoters decided to take the gamble with us this year and agreed to do a 20-date tour of America with us. And the business we've done everywhere has been *tremendous*. We kicked the ass of every other festival out there this summer. " 1997

" I've been lucky enough to get 14 great bands to tour with me this summer. Pantera are a fucking great live band! And like him or not, Marilyn Manson is an entertainer. I think he needs to buy a new pair of tights, though... Fear Factory, Neurosis, Coal Chamber, they're all great live bands. I want to thank everyone that performed with me, because without them there never would have been an OzzFest. " 1997

THAT OL' BLACK MAGIC

On The 2001 Album Sessions

"We all sat down and said, 'It's gotta be the same way as it was before', but it wasn't, you know? I'm not the same anymore, neither are they, you know? I mean, when we started writing, it wasn't the same vibe. I'm used to being a bandleader... I mean, I'm used to having a solo career rather than being a singer with a band. Since I left Black Sabbath, I've never had a band like Black Sabbath, where everyone was equal – it was my solo project, and I had outside help to do writing, so I had the last say on it all, you know?

"People say, 'It was so cool to see you guys back onstage again, and blah, blah, blah, blah, blah, blah, blah.' But I can now rest my head and say, 'We rounded off the rough edges.' When I say that, I mean that we buried the hatchet. And for whatever reason, I'm glad I did it. And if it comes up again and it's worthwhile doing, then I'll do it again." 2001

"At the beginning of the year we agreed that we'd never really tried to make a new Black Sabbath album and that it was something that we'd each regret if we didn't try. The ideas were there but we knew that it had to be at least as good, but hopefully better, than where we left off. In the end it was kinda like meeting up with your first girlfriend years after and giving her a quickie for old times' sake. It sort of worked but yet it didn't. We couldn't recreate the same attitude. Back in the day we were all fucked up and that was something that we weren't gonna do this time round." 2001

Growing Old Disgracefully

GRAPPLING WITH FATHER TIME

❝20 years ago I thought I'd be good for an album, maybe two, and that'd be the end of it, but here I am still doing as good as I ever was. 'Course I feel older but most of all I feel honoured that kids out there still want to play my form of music – that's the biggest compliment, obviously.❞ **1989**

❝**They say act your age. What they mean is that I should have a big beer belly, a bald spot, a nagging wife and stay in every night watching *EastEnders* with my slippers on. And I'm not doing that either.**❞ 1998

❝I would never consider getting my body pierced. Not my nipples, not my dick, not my tongue, nothing. When I get a new tattoo now I insist on new needles, new ink the lot.❞ **1998**

❝**The beauty of being Ozzy is that it doesn't matter who I get up there with, as long as I get up there.**❞ 1998

❝I'm 50 years of age this year; how is a 50-year-old-person supposed to feel? How are you suppose to behave? People say: "Grow up and act your age"... Occasionally I run into old school friends and I go, 'Fucking hell, man, what happened to you?' Bald and big fucking beer bellies, ulcers, car payments...❞ **1998**

"I'd like to get into painting more, I suppose. I do paint a little now and sketch but that's just to get my head out of my arse." 1995

"How the fuck is a legend supposed to feel? Do they wake up in the morning and go, 'Oh darling, I feel very legend-ly this morning?'**"**

1998

"I'd like to put a stop to how we're fucking up this world. I saw a programme the other day saying how we could do a manned mission to Mars by 2020 – aren't we happy with fucking this planet up enough?" 2001

"This is fucking nuts! As you get older, shouldn't it get a bit easier?**" 2001**

"I fear everything and everybody." 2001

"I really had it easy for the last six years, because all I had to do was the OzzFest.**" 2001**

"A lot of people around me have started to get sick. Call me a hypochondriac, or whatever, but I go for regular physicals, and if I get a funny feeling or a lump in the wrong place, I don't fuck around. Remember Randy Castillo, my old drummer? He got cancer in his neck. He's recovered, but he's had a hard fight back, man." 2001

"I turn 53 this December, and my audience keeps growing. I'm luckier than the luckiest son of a bitch walking the planet.**" 2001**

GROWING OLD DISGRACEFULLY

"If I could change anything about myself, I'd give myself serenity I've been looking for since I was a kid. I was born in fear and I've got many, many demons that affect me on many, many levels. The main reason why I still fall off the wagon now is down to lack of confidence. I still have the odd glass of wine that I shouldn't." 2001

"I've just started my autobiography. I've been dictating to my son who's been helping me on his computer. He's the brains of the family. I can't remember anything. Every now and then I'll meet someone I haven't seen for 10 years and they'll go, 'Remember the night you came round to my house and did so and so?' and I go, 'Oh, fuck, yeah. I forgot all about that' – I've got a lot of research to do." 2000

"I'm getting a star with my name on it put on Hollywood Boulevard. So from 14 Landsdown Road, Birmingham, my name on a star on Hollywood Boulevard – that isn't half bad, is it?" 2001

At Home With The Osbournes

THE TV SHOW

❝What is a functional family? I know I'm dysfunctional by a long shot, but what guidelines do we all have to go by? *The Waltons*?❞

❝**The real fact of the matter is sometimes I look at this TV show and I feel sad.**❞

❝For us, this is how we are. This is the way we live. Like it or not.❞
SHARON

❝**People have said to me, 'You're becoming a parody of yourself,' but I'm not becoming anything but what I am. As you see it is as it was.**❞

❝Suddenly I was doing the show. It wasn't my idea. Sharon is my boss, you know.❞

❝**It's kind of a fucked-up life, really. A rock star is supposed to say 'Get me the Vicodins!' Or 'Run me a bath in fucking Perrier water!' I get fucking dogshit up to the elbows and an earful of fucking abuse.**❞

OZZY *Talking*

OZZY *Talking*

"I love you all. I love you with all my heart. But you're all fucking mad!"

"To be honest with you, a few weeks of it was okay, but then, day in and day out, I did eventually get pissed off a bit. I'd been out on tour being on a pedestal for a year and a half. The last thing I wanted to do was come home to a camera crew."

"I landed in New York after the show had aired, and it was like Beatlemania. I'd be walking down the street in New York, and ambulances were talking to me through their PA systems as I'm walking along. Too weird, man."

"I think people like to look through the keyhole, they get off on it. I'm not taking it to heart, I was happy to play along. To be somewhat blind is to be innocent. If the next series flops, so what? I'm a rock'n'roller, not a TV star."

"The show's already been entered for an Emmy award. It's amazing, it's all moving so quickly."

"I haven't watched one single episode of it yet. I'd just get pissed off. I hate my talking voice, I couldn't bear to listen to it for an episode. It must be weird for the kids, though - everyone looking at them, everyone recognising them. I sat Jack down the other night and I was telling him not to make new friends now - you can never be sure why they might want to befriend you."

"We've had people trying to get in over my garden wall, trying to see in. I'll be honest with you, I'm finding it all a bit scary. I'm suddenly thinking what if they kidnap one of the kids or try to steal my dogs?"

"It's a different kind of fame. People always assume they know you because they've seen you on the television, but being at home with me is obviously different. The perception of it has been weird. Everyone's going to me: 'Oh, you're so funny.' I'm certainly not trying to be."

❝The cameras weren't allowed in my bedroom or bathroom. But as soon as I opened the door they were there, they had cameras all over the house. You opened the door and it was - boom! Lights everywhere.❞

❝**You know, there were times when I just wanted to stretch out and scratch my balls, be myself.**❞

❝You know what I think we should do? We should have a crew come out to the house for a weekend and see how we really act. It'd be like The Real World but with us.❞ JACK

❝Oh, that would be a fucking thing, It's got to get on television. All the weak hearts have to watch it. Good idea, Jack.❞

❝**I know my children drink and mess around with stuff they shouldn't mess around with. It's normal for teenagers to experiment, and I trust their judgement. I know there's certain boundaries they won't cross.**❞ SHARON

"It's not as if we're, like, crack-sniffing, living on the streets, we've run away from home... I think we're pretty level-headed." **KELLY**

"I think Aimee is the normal one. She's like the normal girl on *The Munsters*! She can't handle being around us lunatics all day while she's trying to start her career." SHARON

"I find it so annoying, people asking me if my dad eats bats. At school, almost every day, some retard would come up to me and go, 'So, do you guys eat bats?' And I'm like, 'Yeah, all the time; you should come over, we're having a bat barbecue this weekend.'" **AIMEE OSBOURNE**

"We see it as just an entertaining half-hour that takes place in the present, so I don't think it'll go back into history. Anyway, the Osbournes aren't like that. They live in the present."
MTV PRESIDENT OF ENTERTAINMENT BRIAN GRADEN

"He's Homer Simpson come to life. He can't pretend for the camera - he just is. This isn't fuelling the myth of rock'n'roll. The show is the family. Everybody knows about Ozzy's wild past. The twist is seeing he's a loving family man." **MTV EXECUTIVE PRODUCER GREG JOHNSTON**

"Sharon would tell us about what had happened in her house the night before and we'd be dying with laughter. She actually said 'I keep telling Ozzy we should have cameras at the house because nobody believes what goes on'.
"We've been taken aback by how huge this thing turned out. The first time Ozzy returned to the States after it was shown, a baggage handler came up to him who had no idea about his music and said he was a big fan. Ozzy liked that."
MTV EXECUTIVE PRODUCER GREG JOHNSTON

"We used to have ordinary people doing extraordinary things. Now Ozzy opening a garbage bag makes for compelling TV. As long as you put on even a remotely familiar face, no matter how cheesy

AT HOME WITH THE OSBOURNES

or base, people will watch. This is an unfortunate trend I don't see coming to an end any time soon. You're no longer watching TV for the pleasure of a quality programme. Fun is derived from a guilty pleasure. You're watching something almost enjoying the hating of it instead of the enjoyment. **" NANCY MILLER *ENTERTAINMENT WEEKLY***

"So you're a big fan of *The Osbournes*? Well enjoy the next fifteen minutes, because - despite its current ubiquitous popularity - *The Osbournes* is destined for a very short run. Ozzy is obviously a sweet guy who is charmingly willing to make fun of himself. But to have accomplished all that he has and end up being the butt of tired jokes by every hack newspaper columnist in the country can't be very satisfying. In fact, it's sad."

ROLLING STONE COLUMNIST ANTHONY DECURTIS

"You have to get beyond the sort of dysfunctional aspect. I think there are some very good lessons there that are being transmitted, of not doing drugs, of not doing alcohol. In a weird way, Ozzy is a great anti-drug promotion. Look at him and how fried his brains are from taking drugs all those years and everyone will say, 'I don't want to be like that'. **" FORMER US VICE PRESIDENT DAN QUAYLE**

"My favourite moment was when the camera caught Ozzy falling out of his chair - you could hear the cameraman chuckle!"

KERRY KING, SLAYER

"The best thing about the show is the very real aspect of it all. It shows that, no matter who you are, all families are alike. There's definitely no acting involved, it's all real - and that kicks ass! **" MORGAN LANDER, KITTIE**

"There's no way Kelly or Jack can pit one (parent) against the other. There are no secrets in this family. Better to get information on sex and drugs from parents, from families, than from other kids that may be misinformed. He really does a good job with his kids. In his own subtle way, he's shaping his children." KRISTENE DOYLE, DIRECTOR OF CHILD AND FAMILY SERVICES
AT THE ALBERT ELLIS INSTITUTE, NEW YORK.

"The kids feel totally safe with the parents, doing whatever they want to do, saying whatever they want to say, and expressing whatever they want to feel. I mean, who of us had that luxury?"

MANHATTAN THERAPIST SHEENAH HANKIN

Ozzy Meets George Bush

"Every year the White House organises a function for the press corps - basically 10,000 people in a room eating vast amounts and getting pissed. When Bush made his speech he got up and said 'I'd like to welcome Mr & Mrs Ozzy Osbourne,' then proceeded to mention what his favourite Black Sabbath songs were! The next morning I was thinking 'fucking hell, what an incredible journey. From four teenage lads in Brum to dining with the President.' You couldn't write it!"

AT HOME WITH THE OSBOURNES

The Last Word

WHAT'S THE FUTURE TO BE?

"I'll probably be like Burl Ives when I'm a grandfather, singing 'Paranoid'. When I'm about 50, I'm going to do a heavy metal version of 'There Was An Old Woman Who Swallowed A Fly!'" **1980**

"I thought what a fucking epitaph! I've sold God knows how many millions of records but on my gravestone it'll have 'Ozzy Osbourne, born, died, bit the heads off...' What a fucking legacy! Ozzy Osbourne – the real batman! Hahahaha! I suppose there's one good side to it, at least somebody'll remember me..." 1987

"I'll play 'Paranoid' and 'Children Of The Grave', 'Iron Man', all that, all the way to my dying day. When I'm actually dead. They won't play a hymn at my funeral, they'll just play fucking 'Paranoid!'"

"I'm afraid of the way I'll die. I'd like to die in my sleep. I'd hate to get Alzheimer's. But then again, people with it are oblivious. When you're young, you think you've got years ahead, but as you get older it speeds up. There was a time when I wouldn't get out of bed and I wished a good part of my life away. But once a day is gone, it's gone." 1997

"It's been a long haul and I've done everything there is to do. But for the most part I wonder why have I come through after what I did and others didn't? Some genuine, nice guys didn't make it and then there's me, who's been boozing and snorting coke all his life still swanning around..." **2001**

OZZY *Talking*

"I don't believe in God as a physical thing sat somewhere on a cloud in heaven. I reckon heaven and hell are what we make of life right here on earth. I don't believe in the afterlife, I think when you die you're just simply like a piece of shit that needs flushing away." 2001

"You shouldn't ever let go of your dreams. Mine came true and more. I still have problems with ADD, I still have problems reading with my dyslexia, but I still had a great fucking life. People ask if I could do it all again would I do it differently? Fuck off – I had a ball!" 2001

"I can't believe in one God when there's so many Gods – Muslim, Christian, Jewish. There's all these different Gods, but there's only one world. I believe in sticking another o in the word *God*: I believe in *good*, you know?"

"I fucking hate funerals, everyone's fucking crying – boo hoo hoo! – but whoever's dead can't hear you. If someone has died of natural causes it should be a happy occasion. There are two certainties in life – you pay your taxes and you fucking die." 2001